CHANGE

IS

GOOD

KEVIN TURNER

CHANGE

IS

GOOD

CREATING OPPORTUNITY
AMIDST UNCERTAINTY

ASHLEY DOWN BUSINESS PRESS

Printed in the United States of America. For informaion, address
Ashley Down Business Press P.O. Box 2354, Addison, TX 75001

ISBN: 0-9749839-3-4
ISBN-13: 978-0-9749839-3-6

Ashley Down Business Press books are available for special promotions and premiums. For details, contact Ashley Down Business Press Special Markets P.O. Box 2543, Addison, TX 75001 or via email: inquiries@ADBizPress.com

FIRST EDITION

Publisher's Cataloging-in-Publication
(Provided by Quality Books, Inc.)

Turner, Kevin Lane, 1957-
      Change is good : creating opportunity amidst
uncertainty / Kevin Turner. -- 1st ed.
        p. cm.
        Includes bibliographical references.
        ISBN-13: 978-0-9749839-3-6
        ISBN-10: 0-9749839-3-4

        1. Organizational change. 2. Change (Psychology)
        I. Title.

        HD58.8.T87 2011   658.4'06
                                 QBI11-600214

Printed in the United States of America

20 19 18 17 16 15 14

To My Family For Their Love And Support And For Their Pride
In Everything That I Do

To My Clients Who Have Hewn My Knowledge With Experience

To My Friends Who Encourage And Speak Into
My Life

Table of Contents

Preface

In 2005, my second book, *Fearless Leadership* attempted to lay out one of the many step-by-step process tools of behavior modification that we have successfully developed and deployed with countless client trainees over the years. This book was intended to be an insightful, yet practical guide for business executives and HR managers of their human talent capital.

As effective and timely as that book was to our audience, I have learned and experienced so much more since it first came to print. Additionally, new breakthroughs in the latest brain science have further confirmed our development tools and processes since that book. With this in mind, beginning with the tools and concepts first introduced to the reader in the 2005 book, I have added to, updated, and recalibrated the core message from that book. What is now in your hands is an entirely new, different and much better treatise on the core behavioral underpinnings of change resistance. The same practical and insightful tools from the previous work are included for the reader's benefit in this book. However, this new book, *Change is Good* goes further, much further. *Change is Good* expands on the core concepts first introduced in 2005 with new topics and new insights relevant to the performance and behavior of human capital and the paradigm shifts that must occur within leadership and management if an enterprise is to maximize their valued human assets.

A lot has changed since 2005. The global economy has just weathered one of the greatest downturns since the Great Depression, global competition has risen to previously unknown levels, geo-political uncertainties have intensified, and basic commodity costs are on the rise. All of these factors influence the individual and sum total performance of an organization's human capital; their people. Whether you are reading this book for your own personal development or for that of your team, it is my desire that this book unlocks some of the hidden forces behind human performance so that you will be much better prepared to navigate through and even influence the human performance winds that breeze through your sails, especially as they pertain to the one constant in a healthy, vibrant organization; *change*.

I wish to know that I have accomplished my objectives with this book. So, let me hear from you.

Best Regards,
Kevin Turner
President

email: kevin.turner@TLS-t3.com
http://www.TLS-t3.com
972-233-9998
17300 Dallas Parkway, Suite 3100 | Dallas, TX 75248

INTRODUCTION

Progress
Success

Achievement Requires Change

Growth
Spiritual growth requires change.

Sitting at the McDonald's High School Scholar Athlete of The Week Awards Banquet, my daughter, Maria, one of this night's recipients, is unable to attend. She is already away attending classes at Northwestern University in Evanston, Illinois while I attend this awards banquet on her behalf in Dallas, Texas. There are 52 high school athletes chosen from around the Dallas/Ft. Worth area (population 7 million+) to receive this award and Maria has the distinct honor of being one of the fifty-two high school seniors chosen this year.

The applause from the audience crescendos as awards are accepted. I work hard to hold back the rush of emotion as I reflect back to an earlier time. Who would believe we could be here this evening honoring my daughter. No one who knew Maria just six years earlier would have imagined she would be receiving this honor on this very special evening. Seven years earlier, Maria had a difficult time fitting in, and for a junior high girl, it was almost more than she could handle at the time.

Maria struggled with the fear of rejection, low self-confidence and low self-esteem. She felt self-consciously awkward around her peers. Consequently, she withdrew into shyness and alienation solely out of self-preservation. Her shy demeanor loudly communicated low self-confidence to other pre-teens. In addition to this, Maria was devastated at the beginning of her 8th grade year when she failed to make either 8th grade volleyball team. Because of this, ALL of her friends from her team and school rejected and teased Maria mercilessly throughout the year.

Watching how this affected my daughter, I knew we had to take action. However, I also knew that the worse response would be to publicly defend Maria before her more confident peers. Being a counselor/minister by background and a strategist by nature, Maria and I embarked on a path for her personal change and improvement.

For the next five years I became intimately involved with Maria's athletic and psychological development as she pursued her dream of playing volleyball in college. It is safe to say Maria and I spent at least ten to twenty hours together every week during those five years. As things turned out, it served as a training ground for both Maria *and* me. As a result of our travels and talks together in between all of the volleyball events, Maria and I developed a very special bond. She would open up with me and share some of her inner-most thoughts, insecurities, fears and dreams. Her vulnerability and openness with her feelings and struggles sometimes surprised me.

During those hours together, I was able to give my daughter suggestions and advice. Those suggestions served as tools. Because she trusted the words of her father, Maria began *exercising* those suggestions, or *tools*. As a result, she developed the much needed habits, skills and self-confidence required for social success.

Over the years Maria's social skills progressed rather well. Through those special, private one-on-one sessions between a daughter and her father, this young woman was able to conquer her social ineptitude. She grew to become emotionally healthy with a healthy self-confidence.

She embraced _change!_

How did Maria get from where she was six years ago to where she is today? How did she transform from being shy and socially inept, to being socially comfortable, proactive and confident? She did it with the help of three central elements:

First, her core values and principles. This young woman *chose* certain values and principles to serve as the *pillars* of her life and conduct: honesty, integrity, consideration, and hard work to name just a few.

Second, someone (her parent) took the time to *train* and *reinforce* certain skills (mental, attitudinal, behavioral and physical skills) with her through a "training-over-time" training relationship.

Third, she experienced a final "thrust" of *inspiration* from the life and success of others whose personal experiences served as *models* for her to follow (Walter Payton and the 1985 Chicago Bears, Larry Czonka and the 1972 Miami Dolphins, and Michael Jordon, just to name a few).

These three factors gave Maria the ability to conquer fear's adverse power and time-stealing effect over her thinking and choices and this included the various fears resulting from an environment of constant change. Before this time, her life was harnessed and influenced by the subtle, time-stealing forces of fear. However, once the above three dynamics converged upon my daughter's life, she faced and embraced any and every influence of fear (worry, self-doubt, second-guessing, rejection, etc.) and moved forward proactively through constant change.

As the prospect of change, any change, confronts us, emotions like fear, anger and hopelessness often distract us. Those emotions, absent of basic inner strengths and tools, distract and keep us from being the time-effective, productive people we can be. Some people stand firm in the midst of the emotional distractions. Many others fall. This is why some people see change as an opportunity while so many others perceive it as doom and gloom. How does this happen? The answer lies within one's ability to utilize *time* effectively, both physical **and** mental time, without the distractions brought on by emotions.

For more than thirty years I have assisted business executives, owners, family members, and organizations with numerous personal, people, and business-related issues. The vast majority of the people I've worked with are successful, hard working, well-educated and good at what they do. Many have reached some form of financial, vocational or social success. However, even with their successes, most struggle with some form of the emotion of fear when faced with change. Conquering this struggle requires the need to learn and develop new skills in order to adequately deal with their emotions and resulting behavioral habits.

As people come to me for help, I feel a responsibility to give them *more* than they had when we began. This responsibility translates into a pressure to produce a tangible, substantive result for each and every individual, each team and each organization I work with, *every* time I work with them.

The result of this pressure has been the development of what I call "*tools.*" These tools make the intangible (human emotion and behavior) both concrete and predictable. When exercised or applied in a proper training format (referred to as training-over-time throughout this book), these tools help individuals, teams and whole organizations develop skills required for dealing with time-stealing emotions and their habits. In the face of change, the tools and skills then create the strength and focus to conduct business firmly within one's core values and principles. The end result is reduced turnover, higher morale and motivation, increased productivity, and an increase in performance.

This book introduces a few of the tools (there are over 400 to date) that have proven effective in developing the skills necessary to deal with subtle emotions that surface when facing change. *Change is Good* exposes the time-stealing influences of fear and describes the tools and the training-over-time training model. The tools and the training model, together, conquer the time-stealing behavioral habits and increase human performance. Individuals and groups benefit from these tools through training-over-time. This, in turn develops the internal ability to conquer the influences of fear, and then aligns or realigns them with their core abilities to perform and excel.

Change is Good is written for individuals and organizations who, like my daughter, want to overcome the distracting, time-stealing influences of fear in their thinking and decision-making and become the successful, productive individuals and teams they know they can be. Throughout the book, we show you how to conquer fear in the face of change and realign yourself with your core values and principles. We demonstrate a *training-over-time* method of training that has long-lasting results when compared to the more traditional models of self and corporate improvement, such as many consulting initiatives, various seminars, and most forms of coaching. Additionally, *Change is Good* inspires the reader by providing several real-life examples of people and organizations that have overcome fear's influences.

Now, how did my daughter turn out?

Athletically in volleyball, Maria started playing competitive volleyball a full three to four years *after* her peer group began playing the game. She'd played volleyball before that, but only recreationally, not seriously, competitively. Because of this, Maria was never afforded any of the breaks that come to kids when they start out at an early age with their peer group, show signs of promise and are afforded the opportunity to work with and develop under the best coaches for each age group. Consequently, Maria's dad quickly learned about the game of volleyball and became her personal coach.

For years Maria was behind the top local players of her peer group. Our response to this was to work and practice harder and longer than anyone else. I remember the summer between her 9th and 10th grade school years. While all of her peers were sleeping in, Maria arose early every weekday morning at 6am and would hit the volleyball against the school building wall across the street from our house. She had specific drills to do and she passionately worked through each of those drills every day from 6:30am to 10 or 10:30 am throughout the ten or twelve weeks of summer. Maria arose and did this workout early each morning because the blazing Texas summer heat demanded it. Sleeping in was not an option if she was going to reach her goal; to play volleyball in college and this at a time in Maria's life when making her high school *junior* varsity team was largely in doubt. As you can imagine, people laughed at her dream (but they're not laughing now).

Academically, Maria struggled for many years because of fear's influence on her self-concept and confidence. However, the end effect of constantly facing change and defying emotions came four years ago when having been recruited by and given offers from Northwestern University, Cornell University and Brown University (the last two being Ivy League schools) among others, Maria found that her SAT scores were a full *400 points* below the minimum required by each of these three great institutions for athletic admissions.

With this obstacle before her and with the lessons learned from her previous five years of facing change through multiple athletic obstacles, for five short months Maria directed all of her energies toward building her intellectual base or "mean" and raising her SAT scores. And as improbable as it was, Maria raised her SAT score by 400 points within just five months!

Psychologically, together Maria and I used the device of volleyball, with all of its incumbent adversities relative to her specific situation, to develop personal disciplines and habits that caused her to overcome the negative, adverse affects of fear from her early life. Some will find this hard to believe. But all you have to do is sit down with my daughter today, spend ten minutes interviewing her on any topic you wish and you will quickly realize she is now filled with self-confidence and maturity, all because of the emotional/behavioral skills she developed through her athletic and academic pursuits. She is no longer nearly as distracted by emotions like fear as she once was.

In addition, speaking as one business professional to another, there were far, far more adversities that confronted this little girl in volleyball athletics from day one, up to and through the fall of 2010 than most business professionals typically encounter in a similar five year tract. As a matter of fact, the one true shining moment, void of any and all adversities, was that summer of 2008 when Maria was extended offers from four major universities to come, play volleyball and attend their respective schools. That was a huge, shining moment that made all of the hardships and heartaches of the previous year's worth everything.

And here is the eye-opener; my thirty plus years of business experience tells me that few in the world of business and commerce have *ever* had to encounter the amount of unending, unnecessary adversity that my daughter encountered almost daily throughout this odyssey in competitive girls volleyball. It often astounded me to see the length and depth of the unending adversities that came her way, the vast majority of which came very unnecessarily from unsophisticated, insecure, fear-based coaches, parents and peers, not from the game itself.

Today, Maria is an extremely happy, fulfilled student at Northwestern University. She was elected by her volleyball teammates to serve as the team's freshman representative for the NCAA S.A.A.C. her first year there. Although a back injury in the pre-season of her freshman year ultimately led to Maria's retirement from the game, her determination to conquer her fears, embrace change, and fulfill her dream placed her within one of the premiere academic institutions of the world. Plus, in what was to be Maria's final year in competitive volleyball, she and her team made it to the second round of the NCAA Volleyball Championship Tournament, a feat rarely accomplished by most aspiring athletes.

One final comment. The examples and case studies discussed throughout this book are all true. None are fiction. However, to insure the confidentiality and privacy of our clients, names have been changed to protect and preserve those confidences.

PART ONE

Chapter 1

The Latest in Brain Science;
We Have Phineas Gage to Thank

The content you are about to read and experience within these chapters was compiled from over twenty-five years of practical application in the trenches as human behavior battled with everyday life and business. It did not first originate from a classroom or a laboratory, though at times I would have preferred that it had. The tools, ideas, and experiences conveyed to you through these chapters developed out of need; the need of clients seeking our services. Results, created from the execution, exercise and implementation of these tools, ideas, and experiences, kept us in business.

For years people would ask us how this tool or that tool works, or works so consistently, or works so effectively. I honestly did not know the answer. All I knew was that I simply assigned the tools to the client because:

a. They had a need,
b. We were in the business of providing a service and thus, meeting that need,
c. Our tools consistently worked, met the need, and produced the results desired by our clients,
d. This kept us in business.

That was all I could say in answer to the many questions fielded over the years; until recently. During the past few years I have become a student of Brain Science (my lay term for neuroscience, neurology, neurophysiology, neuroendocrinology, neurocircuitry, and neurochemistry). At so many turns I have been utterly amazed with how current research and findings about the inner workings of the brain and human behavior explains why our tools and systems work and work so well (if this sounds like sales hype, it is not - the English language is limited in its ability to help me convey to you just how remarkable these findings were to me).

In the back of this book, I have included for you an excellent bibliography. I highly recommend that you read every book listed from cover to cover. In the process, you will be changing your own brain, rewiring your neurocircuitry. This is one of the ways in which I changed mine.

For now, I only wish to introduce you to a few concepts before you embark on your journey through this book, *Change is Good*. More in-depth study will need to come at your own hands, in your own time, through additional resources like those listed in my bibliography.

Brain Science Summary

For now, I give you this brain science summary.

First, neurons are brain cells. Brains cells are called neurons. Neurons are electrically charged and when triggered, they release chemicals. These chemicals produce our emotions, felt throughout the entire body.

Your behavior and personality originate from these neurons, or more precisely, from the connections these neurons make between one another. It is the connections between various neurons that define who you are, what you do, how you feel, what you think, and how you react.

Fifty percent, 50%, of your neural connections are genetic, they come with you from the womb. The other 50% develop within you through:

a.   What you learn (mental thoughts), and

b.   What you experience (in the world around you).

Repetition of either an experience or learned knowledge causes specific neurons to fire. Those neurons firing at any given moment look around for other neurons that are firing and they then attach to one another (like attracts like). When this process occurs repeatedly (you experience, say, think, feel, learn the same things over and over), these neuro-connections swell or enlarge, literally physiologically growing the size of your brain in that specific area. This is how your behavioral habits are formed.

Plasticity is a relatively new brain science term (about 100 years old) that refers to the flexibility of the brain to adapt and change. In other words, because your brain has plasticity, it has the ability to change beyond childhood development, all throughout your life. Consequently, you can change the way you think, feel, react, etc., all throughout your life. Yes, 50% of you came from the womb. But the other 50% is always in a constant state of flux or change. And, those parts of your brain which are not regularly utilized are regularly pruned, eliminated (your brain is incredibly efficient). In other words, you lose brain cells when they are not being utilized. Conversely, you have the ability to grow your brain cells merely by utilizing or exercising them.

What all of this means is that *you have the ability and power to change by reconstructing your brain circuitry.* I have witnessed this being done for many years as clients have applied our tools and systems to their circumstantial needs. However, before recently, I never knew how it was being done within the individual, or team.

Cognitive-Behavior Therapy or CBT is simply the application of specifically assigned activities, tools, exercises with a client. It has only been within the past few decades that UCLA scientists discovered that CBT can change the brain. CBT teaches a person how to handle thoughts, feelings, reactions, etc. Over time, as the person exercises control over their thoughts, feelings, and reactions, they literally are reprogramming their brain, their neural connections, and therefore changing their personality, behavior and habits.

And *that* is how you and I have the ability to *change*, change for the better.

How are we able to do this and do animals have this same capability?

The orbital frontal cortex (also called the prefrontal lobe and orbitofrontal cortex) is the portion of your brain that gives humans the ability to change our core behavior. Like animals, other parts of our brain give us our basic instincts, such as survival, arousal, etc. However, what sets humans apart from the rest of the animal kingdom is the size of and therefore the ability of our orbital frontal cortex. Ours is double the size of an ape's orbital frontal cortex, six times that of dogs, and 12 times that of cats. It is that part of you that gives you the ability to exercise your will. And when you do exercise your will, and repeat the process, thought or activity, you create new neural connections and in the process, change your brain, change your thinking.

We Have Phineas Gage To Thank!

Where did all of this recent brain science research begin?

We have Phineas Gage to thank for initiating all that neuroscience has come to know and realize over the past century and a half. Phineas lived as a railroad work-crew foreman during the days when the railroad was to industry what the internet and mobile devices are today; THE growth industry. So work was plentiful and it paid extremely well.

Before Phineas, for centuries experts believed that human behavior, personality and therefore the brain's makeup were set from birth; that we came into this world with a certain genetic makeup and that makeup pretty much controlled and defined our personality and behavior for the duration of our lives.

Phineas Gage shook centuries old foundational beliefs about the brain and human behavior. Phineas was an even-tempered, mild-mannered individual. He was one of those whom everyone enjoyed being with. He was easy to get along with and good company.

One day in September of 1848, while working with his railroad construction crew, 25 year old Gage was adding blasting powder, a fuse and sand into the holes that had been drilled in order to blast the rock away from where the railroad was laying its track. Phineas was using a one inch thick iron tamping rod about 3-feet long to accomplish his task when all of the sudden an explosion rocketed the iron tamping rod straight up and through Phineas' skull, up into the air. The iron rod landed some 80 feet away smeared with blood and brain. The projectile had entered Phineas's lower jaw, swept through his brain, just behind his left eye, and exited through the prefrontal cortex region of his brain.

To everyone's amazement, Phineas spoke immediately after the incident and even walked himself to a wagon, sitting upright for the mile ride back to his lodgings in town. However, things did not bode well for Phineas after his accident. For the next two months he slipped in and out of a coma. However, remarkably, by December Phineas seemed to make a full recovery; until . . .

As it turned out, the accident completely altered Phineas' personality and behavior. So much so that the railroad, who once regarded Gage as a favorite with his men and a capable foreman, would not employ him again because of the changes in his behavior. Where once Phineas had been liked and well received, after his accident the doctor who'd attended to Gage immediately after the accident said that Phineas' balance between his intellectual self and his animal instincts had been destroyed. After the accident, Phineas was difficult to deal with and known to indulge in the filthiest of profanities (which he had not been know for before the accident). Sadly, Phineas Gage died 12 years later in 1860. But his experience forever left its mark on brain science and the understanding of the brain's ability to change (its plasticity) and therefore change behavior and personality.

Today, the iron bar, along with Phineas Gage's skull reside in Harvard Medical School's Warren Anatomical Museum.

self control
focus
vision

Chapter 2

Leadership Through Change; Defined

What does it take to be a leader in the face of change? What qualities are found in this type of leadership that sets one apart from the rest?

One of my colleagues once asked the CFO of an $850+ million telecommunications company to define leadership. After a long pause, this CFO responded with: "A communicator; one who leads others, one who is able to listen and then act on what has been taken in."

My colleague then said, "These qualities are all good and true. However, I want you to consider another definition for leadership, one that encompasses the ability to navigate through change. This definition involves three *internal* skills: self-control, focus and vision."

The CFO responded with eyes widening as an audible "wow" escaped his lips. Suddenly, he saw his organization's need and said, "Our leadership possesses *none* of these qualities. We are the epitome of *no control*. We *spend freely* in areas that cannot produce revenue. We *lack the focus* to be an industry leader. Our senior management is too easily *distracted*. Our vision only covers the next *six months*. We function day-to-day."

Time-Effective Leadership Through Change

If leadership can be defined as those individuals possessing:
* *self-control*,
* the ability to *focus* without distractions, and
* the ability to develop and inspire *vision* and direction,

then what is *time-effective* leadership through change?

For those with leadership responsibility, it means first possessing the internal skills of self-control, focus and vision *and* activating those same skills within the individuals under your leadership. With these skills as your core or base, this type of leader then *navigates* him or herself as well as his or her team *through* the process of change, *hold-*

ing at bay the various emotions of fear that threaten to resist and derail the change process; fear of the unknown, fear of failure, fear of inadequacy, fear of being replaced or displaced, etc.

Interestingly, although for the most part we humans work to *avoid* change, the human body is a laboratory of constant change. As infants, our bodies are changing at the rate of billions of additional cells per day. As we age, cell growth retards and even reverses. However, throughout the life of the human creature, we are constantly *changing*.

So, if we are creatures of constant change, why are we so adverse to change and why aren't leaders capable of leading effectively through change? The answer lies within the dynamics of change and its effect on the *emotions* of the human creature.

Dynamics of change?

Self-Control, Focus and Vision

My son George, was born with the birth defect Spina Bifida. George has spent his life in a wheelchair. He has a shunt (a pump) in his brain to pump the fluids out of his brain and into his abdomen. When this shunt malfunctions, it can cause irreversible brain damage. George's shunt has malfunctioned three times so far in his life. Through all outward appearances, George has not experienced any adverse effects from those malfunctions. However, George struggles with a diagnosed learning disability. So, one cannot help but wonder if the two are connected.

Because of the disequilibrium experienced in his head with the shunt and body fluids, George has always had a tremendous amount of fear with any sensation that remotely resembles roller-coaster rides, swinging high in swings, or being aloft in the air. This fear, left unbridled to rule for so many years, grew and spread to affect many other areas of George's life. Consequently, irrational fear gripped much George's life until recently. These fears, coupled with his learning disability, greatly limited George in every facet of life and relationships.

Struggling miserably with his academics, three years ago George approached me one day and asked, "Will you do the same thing for me that you did for Maria (see Introduction for details)?" George saw how his sister *transformed* in core personality, right before his eyes, as Maria walked through her own process of change. Now, imprisoned by his own fears, his learning disability, *and* living with the miserable results of both, George *wanted change* and was now willing to do whatever he had to in order to experience that change, regardless of the fear. With that, George and his dad embarked on George's own journey out of fear into a productive, fulfilling life.

Our first order of business was to change George's approach to his academic studies. George had tremendous test anxiety and fear of failure every time he turned in any assignment. Consequently, George's fear caused him to self-destruct and sabotage the very result he worked so hard to obtain.   False Evidence Appearing REAL

Face Fear Head-On

The only way to conquer fear is to face it head-on. So, George learned how to:

a. schedule and *plan out* his entire semester's work/study schedule on a weekly calendar, at the *beginning* of each semester, *well ahead* of any due dates,

b. figure out where the professors placed the *value* on each assignment, exam, etc., which allowed George to *project* out to the end of the semester and capture a ***vision*** of what his final grade would or could be possibly be,

c. *manage* and *proportion* his study *time* according to the values of all of the various assignments; quizzes, homework, tests, projects, papers, class participation, etc.,

d. *think* while reading content,

e. take *highlights* while reading,

f. *save time* by skim-reading where and when possible,

g. *prepare*; study and re-study his highlights *weeks before* his tests and exams.

Next, George simply made himself, exert ***self-control***, to follow his plan. This caused George to stay ***focused*** and not be so easily distracted by his emotions (fears).

With this new approach, George spent eight to twelve hours studying almost every day. Why? Because he was *driven* to reach his *vision* (established early in the semester). Whereas in the past, without a vision, George was easily and constantly distracted by emotions, fears, impulse gratification, etc. And this always bore fruit with disastrous consistency. Now, with this new formula, George gained the ability to remain focused until the final bell was rung, until the job was done.

Consequently, George's grades improved substantially, even in spite of a diagnosed learning disability. More than that, George acquired some new internal strengths: self-control, the ability to focus, and the ability to develop a vision that would lead him to achieve what he never before was able to achieve; results commiserate to his efforts.

George's transformation culminated in the Spring of 2011 when George's university, the University of Arkansas, held its first ever Disabilities Awareness Week. George was the designated leader of this event. The university's Chancellor, Dr. G. David Gearhart, appointed George with the responsibility to create, organize, and conduct a Disabilities Awareness campaign for his university. Dr. Gearhart appointed several school administrators to serve over George and the event as an Advisory Committee, including the Dean of Students and the Head of the Center for Educational Access department.

It was a huge success. Beginning in November, George started organizing and planning the entire event, regularly submitting his ideas, planning and progress to his Advisory Committee. In January and February George recruited over one hundred student volunteers to help with the event. He then interviewed, selected, and trained the top 16 to serve on four committees he created, and appointed Committee Chairs over each of these four.

George did not stop there. He also went to the major departments and recruited their support (the Athletic Department, the Business School, the Student Government Association, etc.). George then also recruited financial support from local and National merchants and all of the University's Dorm Hall Senates. George went so far as to write letters to the CEOs of every major automobile manufacturer requesting their support for the event. To everyone's surprise, the Executive Assistant to the CEO of General Motors called George personally to voice their support.

In March, six weeks before the event's date, George turned the daily operations of the entire event all over to his Committees and the committee chairs and he moved into a management role. Through this entire project, change was the *one constant* George could count on. Unfazed, George moved with the flow at every turn. It was truly amazing to witness George's leadership skills running full throttle without the past distractions of fear and the fear of change.

Leadership is *not* a position or title. Leadership is *not* a list of external qualities. Yes, effective leaders should possess external attributes like the ones our CFO friend mentioned earlier or the ones my son George exhibited. However, external abilities are the *result* or fruit, not the core or *root* of time-effective leadership through change.

The dynamics that drive time-effective change leadership, regardless of title or position, are *internal*, not external, in nature. They are the internal skills of self-control, focus and vision and are at the core of time-effective leadership. This core serves as the springboard, the launch-pad that gives you the ability to successfully bridle the emotions and navigate through change.

Leadership potential resides within most of us. However, it often lies dormant because of the distracting influences of fear, *especially fear as it reacts to change*. What can activate this potential? The development of the internal ability to conquer the distracting influences of fear, and then the alignment or realignment of the individual with his or her core values and principles. This ability grows out of the *acquired* skills of self-control, focus and vision.

Internal Leadership Skills Are Learned

The internal skills necessary to lead time-effectively through change are mostly *acquired* behaviors and habits; mental, verbal, physical, and emotional habits. In other words, if you or your people do not currently possess them, these skills can be developed through performance training-over-time, a training method explained later in this book. Consequently, you and your team have the potential of seeing these behaviors activated within yourselves, individually and collectively, to such a degree that it affects your *culture*.

A survey conducted in 2010 by the Harvard Business Review revealed that *thirty-three percent* of "high-potential" employees admitted to *not* putting all their effort into their job. If this is the case, can we realistically conclude that with just a few adjustments we can dramatically affect people's time-effectiveness and performance through change?

What would happen if during the next eighteen months, your company's productivity increased substantially as a *direct* result of affecting your "high potentials" productivity? If the full leadership potential is developed and awakened within your "high-potential" talent pool, then isn't it realistic to expect a dramatic increase in productivity, morale and talent retention? This in turn leads to a dramatic increase in growth, revenue and market share.

For your organization, leading through change can mean:

- · More motivation.
- · More innovation from within.
- · More business opportunities.
- · Reduced turnover.

- · Increased energy.
- · Greater efficiencies.
- · Increased market share.
- · Increased productivity.

Activating Leadership Potential

The key to success relies on the activation of the leadership potential within yourself first, and then your people, regardless of their position. This then, requires you to lead the entire group to function as a team. And this means creating and developing an entire organization characterized by people who epitomize time effectiveness, collaborative change management, and maximum team performance: self-starters, self-motivators, people who consistently take initiative, people who collaborate across functions and departments rather than compete cross-functionally, and those who account for the distractions of fear in the face of change, *all* of these are *attributes of leadership*.

A plethora of written documentation is readily available that supplies us with facts and data affirming the economic benefits of putting an organization's human capital first. In addition, business history affirms that a people-centered strategy is a sound economic business approach. Dean Foods, Southwest Airlines, Google, TDIndustries, The Container Store and many others are examples of this. These organizations are consistently fiscally profitable, primarily because of their people-centered approach to their businesses.

If this is correct, then why aren't more businesses developing the maximum potential of their human capital? Scores of executives claim that they and their organizations are people-centered. However, peering beyond the rhetoric, most rely on outdated "old-school" tactics and ineffective strategies that simply do not work. With such consistently poor results, one would think that these leaders would abandon their old methods and embrace an authentic people-centered approach of collaborative change management if only they knew how. This notion then begs the question, "Why doesn't leadership know *how* to execute such a people-oriented, change strategy?" Maybe it is because they lack an understanding of the core of human performance and behavior – the intersection of human emotion with one's self-control, focus and vision, and in particular, the emotion of fear.

Leadership Amidst Change

Leaders are not born. They are made. Everywhere we look we see a *shortage* of leaders who can time-effectively lead through change. Currently, there is *no* shortage of people inadequately suited to fill leadership positions. But there *is* a shortage of people who function time-effectively in the role of leadership through change. There is a deficiency of time-effective leadership that knows *how* to activate the leadership ability and potential within themselves and within each of their people. The reason for this is often rooted in distracting emotions like fear. Leadership may be afraid to give their people the freedom to act on their own ideas, or there may be a fear culture within that restricts them from offering their ideas.

The right tools, channeled through training-over-time, develop the skills necessary for time-effective leadership through change. The old adage is true: choices make the person. Choices either make or break one's leadership potential. Remember:

> *Sow a thought, reap a deed.*
> *Sow a deed, reap a habit.*
> *Sow a habit, reap a destiny."*

It all begins within the human mind, where emotion and core values intersect. However, all too often, fear steals valuable, critical time and restricts or controls a person's decision-making faculties.

What, then, is time-effective leadership through change? It is leadership that is *not* controlled by the time-wasting influence of emotions like fear. The emotion of fear is a major, often hidden force in life. Leaders of change recognize these influences on themselves and the people they lead. They also understand how fear affects behavior, time usage and decision-making, and they then counteract those influences by developing basic internal skills within themselves and those under their leadership. The remainder of this book addresses these issues and presents a set of practical tools and strategies for developing a leadership style that is time-effective through change.

Chapter 3

Fear of Change in the Workplace

On the surface, this particular Fortune 500 technology organization (we'll call them Company A) was similar to other major players in the global marketplace. Characterized by steady growth over two decades, it once was an industry leader within its sector. To all those looking in, Company A seemed poised to lead its industry into the 21st century. Although sales from their primary product line had reached a plateau, Company A was reinventing itself in a clear attempt to remain at the top of their industry.

The strategy was for Company A to create a special division for the sole purpose of expanding its product line with a value-added service. This new service fit nicely with the explosive growth of the telecommunications industry, within which Company A was beginning to lose traction.

Although Company A's new value-added service had a clear niche within the marketplace, sales were negligible. Growth with this new division was stagnant. My firm was asked to assess the problem and evaluate the effectiveness of the organization's regional sales teams throughout the U.S.

It didn't take us long to discover the problem. As a matter of fact, we noticed it as we walked in the door of the organization's headquarters. It permeated every fiber of Company A. However, the employees were so heavily dominated by the problem's power that no one recognized its existence. It is often that way for those on the inside – they can't see the forest for the trees.

What was this hidden power? What was it that permeated, influenced and controlled the people of Company A like an unspoken cultural creed? What was it that was adversely affecting the growth and survival of this organization? It was the fear of change. More specifically, it was a culture of fear, intimidation and control.

Leaders Use the Fear of Change

Fear of change (change resistance) is one of the most, if not *the* most familiar bedfellows for many organizations within the marketplace today. Pressured to produce quick results, leadership often turns to fear tactics because such tactics usually produce quick results, *and* because they know of no other way. Leaders use fear to motivate, delegate and eradicate. Subordinates submit to it knowingly and unknowingly, because they have so much riding on their jobs – namely their income, identity and future.

The power of corporate fear is so intoxicating that people adapt to its presence, unknowingly altering their thinking and behavior. Consequently, long-term performance is suppressed. People don't perform their best when performing out of fear. Much of their time is wasted while factoring in all of the potential risks or consequences of a given decision. Then even more time and energy is spent covering their backsides from potential adverse reactions to their decisions by their superiors. Forget creativity or unique ideas. It isn't worth the risk.

The result? Valuable, critical time is lost. Innovation is squelched. Productivity is restricted. All because of the emotion of fear.

Fear At The Top

Corporate fear is a cultural problem that can begin at the top of an organization. So, why do some leaders use fear tactics to produce results from those under their leadership? From the outset, incoming leaders know they are expected to produce results *immediately*. Their marching orders are clear. They have only a few months to demonstrate their ability and produce results, or market forces will find someone else who can.

Because of this pressure, it doesn't take long for one in leadership to see the power that fear can have on one's subordinates to produce results. In the immediate, fear motivates people to work hard, try harder, produce and/or do something more or different. Before long, with fear as the fuel, some leaders learn to rely on this slash-and-burn technique of business management, simply because it generally produces quick results.

On the other hand, leaders can choose to conquer fear's power by determining to develop and increase their people skills, their tactical skills, and their time-effective leadership ability to lead themselves and their people through change. However, on the front end this requires time and hard work, and some are not willing to pursue this option.

Often, the slash-and-burn management style leads people to make compromises of character or principles. For the short term, productivity may go up (because of unscrupulous sales techniques, inventive accounting, or the pressure to get results at all costs), but morale goes down. Outwardly, everyone wears a smile. Inwardly, many battle with their conscience.

This leadership style wreaks havoc on those caught in its intricate web. Although people come and go, productivity is able to sustain itself, for a while, as long as there is always a fresh crop of new blood to run through the system and produce the numbers. This is fear's legacy.

A fear-based management style is doomed in today's environment. *Only those companies with leaders that have the talent and ability to strategically lead and motivate their people through change, apart from the tactics of fear, are the ones that thrive and survive over the long haul.* Fear does not lead, it manipulates. There is a big difference between leadership and manipulation. One possesses endless potential. The other always ends in destruction, decay or death. One is endless. The other is an end in itself.

When people make compromises, the compromises add up. Why? Because compromising your character violates your conscience. The governing principle behind this dynamic is, *"We reap what we sow"* If you sow good, you will reap good. When you sow bad, it always comes back on you somehow, someway, some time, no matter how hard you work to avoid it. The collapse of the banking and financial system in 2008 is proof-positive of this.

Company A was a cesspool of fear in the workplace. Our assessment work confirmed this. Drastic changes were required in order to change that organization's course. Can such change occur? Yes. However, it requires a *commitment* to change and the *time* to see it through to completion and all of this must begin at the top. From there, it then requires practical tools through a training-over-time human performance change model to produce genuine attitudinal behavior, productivity, and cultural change.

In the case of Company A, no one at the top would stop long enough from the day-to-day pressures to commit to a program of

change. Consequently, within months of our prognosis Company A
filed for bankruptcy and was eventually bought out by a competitor
for pennies on the dollar. However, a buyout did not fix the problem.
The competitor unknowingly inherited the original cultural disease.
Within 18 months the competitor filed for bankruptcy as well, due in
part to the cultural problems they inherited from Company A.

Fear's Grip on Leadership

Ineffective leadership not only leads others by using manipulation
and fear tactics, they also allow the fear of change to negatively affect
their own performance. Consider the following situation.

A senior vice president makes a mis-hire. The new employee is
ruining inter-office relations, alienating everyone he comes into contact with. The new-hire's job requires daily interaction with the very
people that he is alienating. People are whispering among themselves.
Everyone's productivity slides as their focus is distracted by the new-
hire. Morale and productivity are shrinking across the board.

What does the senior VP do? Get coaching or training for the mis-
hire? Terminate the mis-hire? Re-position the mis-hire? Or better
yet, do nothing and hope everything works out, all the while watching
as several of his key "high-potential" people leave because of an inability to work with this problematic performer?

The above scenario is played out day after day all across the
globe. Why doesn't the senior VP act decisively, before the mis-hire
runs off some of his key, top talent, costing the organization as much
as $377,000 per "high-potential" employee (see below figure) in re-
placement costs?

The answer is often rooted in the fear of change. Let's look at each
option from the perspective of this senior VP.

1.   Get coaching or training for the mis-hire.

First there is the senior VP's supervisor. What will he or she think
of the senior VP and his ability to recruit, interview and hire good
people, especially if this isn't his first mis-hire (and it typically isn't
since the average mis-hire rate currently stands at 50%)? Such an
expenditure as coaching or training so early into the mis-hire's tenure
will quickly reveal the senior VP's inability to select solid talent and
therefore have dire consequences on his superior's trust in his abilities
and therefore, his upward mobility.

Because of this, the senior executive finds himself functioning more out of self-preservation than out of instinct and skill to perform his role and provide the best for his team and organization, even after this hiring miscue. *Self-preservation is a by-product of the fear of change.*

Second, how would the senior VP approach the mis-hire about coaching or training? What would this communicate to the newly hired employee? How would the mis-hire respond to this proposal? Again, red flags, rooted in fear, worry and concern hinder the senior VP from decisively and quickly addressing the problem.

2. *Terminate the mis-hire.*

This definitely is a non-option for four reasons.

First, it wouldn't look good on the senior VP's track record to have hired and then terminated a person so quickly. Admission of making such a costly mistake is taboo. Both peers and superiors will lose confidence and respect in him and his ability. They will see him as weak or inadequate in his role (or so he fears) and some will then attempt to take advantage of that.

Second, the current talent pool is already lean. The senior manager's department is understaffed. Consequently, he cannot make a decisive move, out of a fear of creating an even bigger problem with his department's productivity.

Third, the costs involved with the termination, hiring and training process are too high to be repeating the whole process again (these costs at Company A were conservatively figured to be over $377,000 *per* regional sales manager).

Fourth, he could risk legal action by the one being terminated.

3. *Re-position the mis-hire.*

Of all options, this seems to be the best. Place the mis-hire somewhere else within the organization in order to get him or her out of the way. Trade them for another person. Let the mis-hire be someone else's problem.

That helps the organization, doesn't it? The senior executive reasons within himself how this can be a win-win for everyone. Again, he is acting out of self-preservation rooted in the fear of change.

4. *Do nothing and hope the problem goes away.*

This option is usually the pick-of-the-litter.

Why? Because it is the easiest. How? It's easier to do nothing. Doing nothing requires no action or effort. You do not have to worry about the effects of change when there is no change made. Just firmly entrench your head in the sand and move forward, right?

Consequently, with this option, major negatives surface within the senior VP's department. Key, "high-potentials" transfer or leave the firm all together. This results in a further erosion of morale, and decreased productivity.

The senior VP now finds himself spending the bulk of his time *positioning* and *posturing*, as opposed to *performing* the tasks for which he was hired. He becomes a one-man PR campaign for himself and his own position. The senior VP is always looking for scapegoats and excuses to deflect problems away from his leadership ability, while at the same time trumpeting anything and everything good about himself and his work.

Do you see how the fear of change (change resistance) can affect a person when considering just *one* wrong decision? Do you see how much company *time* is lost to such back-end protection? Can you imagine how much more time-effective and productive this senior VP would be if fear did not influence or control his thinking, his judgment or his performance? Take a moment to go back and review this story. At each step of the way, do a rough calculation of the *time* this senior VP most likely spent (or wasted) on contemplating his dilemma. Add up the figures you come up with. Now, how much more productive could this senior VP's time have been if that block of time were directed toward real business problems or real business opportunities with real business solutions? The answer is often eye-opening.

Before we look at how to conquer workplace change resistance and eliminate its time-wasting influence from our performance, let's explore some additional ways that change resistance impacts a company's bottom-line. The next chapter describes how people allow the emotion of fear to lead them into compromises of integrity, with negative results for both the individual and the organization.

Chapter 4

How Fear Compromises Integrity

The competitive spirit is more alive today than ever before. Globalization forces every business entity to raise the bar of competition and performance. Technology and the Internet force us to compete on levels that were unheard of just a generation ago. Wireless innovations are challenging executive boards to re-think and re-evaluate their organization's strategy, focus and mission.

Competitive pressures entice people to compromise. This is sometimes good for business. Making a compromise of *position* for a win-win outcome is usually beneficial. Often, however, compromises involve a compromise of *integrity*, character or values, not simply a compromise of position. Why does this happen? Why do people compromise their principles? Usually, it is because they succumb to the emotion of fear.

Change resistance that stems from fear entices people to make decisions that contradict their character. Under normal circumstances, they would never consider such a choice. But out of fear and the pressure it unloads on them, they do it anyway.

What kind of fear creates this type of pressure? Fear of failure, fear of impending doom, fear of being replaced or displaced, fear of losing, fear of being inferior or inadequate, and the fear of change; each can trigger the enticement to compromise.

There is also the fear of death – death of an organization, death of a livelihood, death of a career, death of an image, and death of a dream. Consequently, people and organizations compromise their integrity not only to succeed, but also to survive. Or so they believe.

Do we need to make these compromises of character? Fear often tells us yes. In reality, however, the answer is no. There always are other alternatives.

Consider the following examples of how fear compromises sound judgment and ultimately results in a negative effect on the company and/or the individual.

Fear of Failure

Dozens of start-ups like Grocery.com and Alta Vista were darlings of the Internet boom. At one point, their respective stock price reached dizzying heights. However, the great bear market of 2001 brought many of those companies down to earth and even out of business.

How does fear factor into this? During the early stages of their explosive growth, flush with investor's cash, the leadership of many start-ups made an all-too-common mistake: early expansion.

Often, companies experiencing initial success with a single product or service feel the need to expand their product or service line too quickly. Why? The emotion of fear.

Once euphoric with the initial success, instead of strengthening their single, successful service or product line, an organization's leadership will worry (a milder term for fear) that they will lose market share. So what do they do? Boldly, they expand into other arenas of business.

Then what happens? As in the case with so many of the internet darlings, most early expansion efforts are met with failure. Why? Because the leadership stretches the organization's resources too thin, too early in the game, consequently weakening the organization.

So, by giving in to the fear of losing market-share, a company expands too quickly, just after reaching initial success with one product or service. With early expansion come increased demands on every already stretched-thin resource, both capital and human. When the organization has certain weaknesses, such as:

- lack of experience in the new areas of expansion, or
- untimely product introduction, or
- miscalculation of the market need, or
- under-capitalization, or
- under-staffing, or
- vulnerability to economic or market shifts,

the very thing they feared – failure – was brought upon them as a result of stretching their resources and capabilities too thin, too fast.

Falling to Fear

Why do so many fall to fear?

The need to succeed or survive creates internal pressure. Excessive internal pressure creates negative emotions, such as worry, panic, anxiety and fear. The negative emotions then pressure people into making decisions in an attempt to relieve the pressure. The result? Usually a bad, untimely, or wrong decision that ultimately affects their career, the department, and/or the organization.

The Enron fallout is an example of this dynamic. Why did the leadership of this Fortune 500 company willfully choose to create and maintain so many different offshore entities? Why did top Wall Street banks deem it necessary to label last minute loans to Enron as "commodity transactions" rather than loans? While their greed was the initial propellant, their goal became misdirection. The thrusting force behind that goal was fear; fear of being caught, exposed. The result was collapse and ruin for everyone caught in the wake of this corporate giant.

All of this misdirection reminds me of an infamous U.S. president who took the art of misdirection to a new level. When reviewing tapes of past interviews, especially ones with pointed, direct questions about his fidelity, we see how this president craftily answered questions in ways that, on the surface, seemed to have answered the interviewer's questions. However, knowing what the public now knows, if we review for a second time his answers to those questions, we see that he was using the tool of misdirection. Most people call this a lie disguised as a truth. Why do people do this? Fear. Fear of being caught or found out. Fear of failure.

In hindsight we can see the devastation that the fear and greed of a few has on the lives and careers of so many. In the case of Enron, on the surface we only see the collapse of Enron and its accounting firm, Arthur Andersen. However, the ripple effect is powerful. Retired school teachers lost their retirement funds which were invested in Enron stock. Small business vendors of either Enron or Andersen struggled to fill the hole left by these two giants.

And if you think this was an isolated instance, we need only to look at the more recent housing bubble and subsequent burst to see how fear, initially propelled by greed, is still at work in the marketplace today. It is so interesting how the fear of change will paralyze a person into indecision, but greed will propel them. And then, once greed has thrust an individual into action, subsequent fears lead them into all sorts of irrational and illogical decisions and behaviors. This entire progressive process is fascinating and it is a weak side of human nature, all set forth by change resistance, the fear of change.

When a person or an organization in a position of leadership succumbs to fear, the consequences are magnified and devastating. Many are affected when it involves a leader. Low morale within an organization is often a tell-tale sign of fallen integrity within an organization. Why? Because a leader, by the very nature of his or her position, has followers. People look to the leader not only for vision and direction, but also for trust, integrity and example. People want their leaders to model a higher conduct for all to aspire to, respect, and follow. For this reason, leadership shoulders higher responsibilities in more ways than one.

Ignoring Instinctive Fear — Some Fear is Good

While some people fall to the influence of unfounded fears, others ignore a healthy, instinctive fear that is designed to warn them of impending dangers. The following story illustrates how this occurs.

"Ready in three, two, one," the television floor producer shouted as he pointed to me and the news anchor. With that, the anchor began our interview. I was asked to answer the question, "Why do people cheat on their spouses?" Not a typical business topic, but it was the hot topic of the moment. The day before this interview, a nationally known figure was exposed for being embroiled in extra-marital affairs. Looked up to and supported by millions, many were deeply hurt, angered and disappointed.

As the television station's "Corporate Coach and Relationship Expert," the news anchor turned to me and began, "You recently met this man. Did you know this was going on?"

"No," I responded, "I don't think anyone knew. That's why it caught so many by surprise. He's a highly respected figure worldwide. Consequently, this news hurts and disappoints a lot of people."

With that response, the interviewer sat up erect in her seat, "If that is so, then how could this have happened? How could he have done this?" Her facial features took on a more serious tone at this point. "Why do people cheat," she asked?

Quickly, I responded, "Why would any of us cheat? There are several reasons. The first reason is that we all have *needs*; be they physical, emotional, or intellectual. When our basic needs go unmet, we are much more susceptible to any form of enticement. The second reason is that we rarely *pre-plan* for those unforeseen times when enticement catches us off-guard. We all are only one step away from a similar fate. For this reason we need to pre-plan. How many times have you pre-planned for your weaknesses or shortcomings; be they physical, emotional, or intellectual? Successful individuals and organizations do. We need to have an offensive *and* a defensive strategy that further protects us from our own weaknesses. A third reason for cheating is that we sometimes ignore our *instinctive fears*. Everyone is equipped with an instinctive fear. This is a good fear. It protects us from potential problems, such as the instinctive fear that warns us not to jump off of a cliff or tall building. When we do not heed this fear's warning, doom and disaster are typically just around the corner."

The basic emotion of fear is so wide-spread and for this reason most of us are unaware of its work and influence on our thinking and choices. We may not even be sure how to recognize fear in its various forms. The next chapter helps us recognize some of the different forms of fear and its effect on our lives.

Chapter 5

Recognizing Fear

My CEO friend had a problem. Sitting in his office, the door closed behind us, he leaned toward me across the large rosewood desk and said, "Kevin , I really need your help. Ron (one of the company's senior vice presidents) is after my head. I can't prove anything, but I know something is going on. I can feel it. He's trying to entrap me. What do I do? How do I deal with this?"

Leaning back in my chair, I looked him straight in the eye and said, "Tell me, John, how well are you doing your job these days?" He didn't say anything, but he didn't have to. I already knew the answer. When you become distracted by fear, when you focus on something other than your job or your responsibilities, your productivity and performance diminish. It doesn't matter whether the fear is legitimate or not. It grabs your attention, and doesn't let go.

"All right," I said, "let me ask you something else. When you are fully attentive to your job, when you're making full use of *all* your talents and abilities, how productive are you?" He had moved up through the ranks to become CEO of this large and successful company, so I wasn't at all surprised when he shrugged and answered, "One hundred percent."

"Now tell me," I went on, "how productive have you been lately?" He thought for a moment, shook his head, and said, "Probably forty percent."

"And what happens," I asked, "if you continue functioning at forty percent?" At first he looked somewhat confused, as though he hadn't understood the question. But as the significance of the answer dawned on him, he began nodding his head. "Of course," he said, "of course. If I spend all my time worrying about Ron instead of doing my job—which is exactly what I've been doing—I'll lose no matter what he does!"

Unfortunately, this is an excellent example of how fear affects an individual, from one as successful as the CEO of a company to a mid-level manager of a team or department. What my questions enabled John to recognize was that *fear makes us behave in ways that we wouldn't otherwise behave.* If he hadn't been afraid of being displaced, and simply continued doing as he always had, his continued success would have been more than sufficient to counter any political attack. However, because he'd become preoccupied with and therefore distracted by the idea that Ron was trying to ruin him and his career, his performance dropped dramatically.

Ironically, as a result, John was actually providing ammunition to *anyone* who might wish to undermine him, be it Ron, a Board member, or anyone else. How? Because John was not 100% sure that Ron was out to get him. John was acting on what he *felt*, not what he *knew* by fact. His emotions could have been misleading him to faulty assumptions. And those faulty assumptions could then have been mis-leading John to alter his own behavior in ways that hurt his performance and subsequently jeopardize his career.

Fear

Do you recognize fear in your thinking? Can you identify fear's effect on your choices? Some people say that fear does not affect them. That's not surprising. The vast majority of those controlled by fear are unaware of its influence on their words, actions, thoughts and behaviors. However, if you have ever caught yourself thinking or feeling any of the following emotions, then chances are that fear influences your decision-making and time-effectiveness:

Nervous	Anxious
Worried	Panicky
Concerned	Butterflies
Conservative	Insecure
Cautious	Inferior
Careful	Uncertain
Doubtful	Unsure

Before you can work on controlling and conquering the fear in your life, you must first learn to recognize what fear looks like and understand how it works.

Two Types of Fear

Fear isn't necessarily a bad thing. Some fear is good! There are essentially two types of fear; *instinctive* fear and *unfounded* fear. Interestingly, both are influenced by our social conditioning. However, there is a very important difference between them. Instinctive fear is the sort of fear we might feel if we are walking alone down a dark city street one night and suddenly hear footsteps behind us. We know that sometimes people in such situations get attacked, and it is our instinctive fear that warns us to be careful and on-guard. It is also our instinctive fear that keeps us motivated and on the right path, such as when we use our fear of going to prison as a motivation to obey the laws. For very obvious reasons, instinctive fear is valuable.

Unfounded fear, however, is almost never valuable, but limiting and time-wasteful. While it too is based on our social conditioning, it is also based on assumptions formed from our social knowledge or past experiences but has no basis in fact. For example, chances are good that when you were a child, you learned how to ride a bicycle. Learning to ride isn't necessarily easy, but most of us persevere and eventually are able to do it. Let's say, though, that in the process of trying to learn, you fell and bruised yourself so many times that eventually you just gave up. Now it is years later, your children are riding their bikes around the neighborhood, and your spouse suggests that you learn to ride so you can all ride bikes together. But you can't do it. In fact, you're afraid to even try, because you are convinced by your past experience as a child that you'll never be able to learn how to successfully ride a bike and therefore will fail. That's an unfounded fear and yet, although it may not be a bike, there are a lot of past experiences in people's lives that cause them to conclude they will fail if they ever try again. Consequently, they are doomed to fail because they don't even try.

Let's look at some examples of both kinds of fear.

Instinctive Fear

Instinctive fear that warns us of real and impending problems is a good fear. When we heed this type of fear, it keeps us, our families, and our businesses alive to fight the fight for another day. It enables us to survive. It protects us from our own weaknesses and blind spots. This type of fear is an inborn trait found within every human.

Instinctive fear is a natural self-protective mechanism. Like any strength or power, however, instinctive fear has the ability to mushroom into a disproportionate, out-of-control state – so much so that it engulfs our consciousness, controlling our thinking and performance.

Strategic planning, whether organizational or personal, should always factor in the forces of fear, especially the fear of change and change resistance, within the organization's talent pool.

Without a healthy dose of instinctive fear, we would jump off a building or mountain and kill ourselves while seeking a short-term adrenaline rush. Or we would lie, cheat, and steal to triumph over our competitors. However, many of us allow unfounded fear to grow out of balance to the degree that it distracts our focus, thus affecting our time-effectiveness, performance, and our ability to work through change.

Very few of us (I believe the figure is 10 to 20%, based on my thirty-plus years of experience) learn how to control fear, listen to real or instinctive fear and use it for a competitive advantage. Most people unknowingly allow fear to influence their thinking, choices and career, *or* they go to the opposite extreme and ignore it all-together. Both approaches always lead to diminished returns.

An awareness of your instinctive fear signals also allows you to successfully take on more calculated risks. What is risk-taking? It is the bridling of fear in order to move forward toward a hoped for, unrealized goal or objective. Those who are consistently successful with taking calculated risks are able to harness fear to their advantage. Change is easier for them.

A good friend of mine once told me that he uses fear to motivate him to *positive* action. This friend has built an incredible organization. Beginning with just a few people and one service-product in 1990, he has masterfully built this organization into one of the largest of its kind in the world. His organization has been recognized time and again for having had one of the fastest growths during the past twenty years.

Through it all, I have been amazed with my friend and his staff. From day one, they seem to live on the cutting edge, making decisions on the fly, not wasting time worrying about or contemplating all of the possible negative consequences. They remain focused on their vision, exercising self-discipline and not allowing anything, including fear, to distract them from their ultimate objective.

Out of sheer respect and awe for what this organization has accomplished, I asked him one day about the growth. As I listened to his answer, it became obvious that *decisiveness* was a key part of his strategy. Out of intrigue, I asked the one question that interested me the most, *"Does fear ever affect you or your decision-making?"*

Immediately he responded, "Yes, definitely. *Fear motivates me.* I turn the negative of fear into a positive influence for change. Consequently, we are able to *embrace change.* So, I use fear in positive ways."

Wow! Here is an example of one leader choosing to *not* allow fear to control him, distract his focus or affect the execution of his vision. Instead, he uses the negative force of fear for good. He uses fear to provide a motivation for positive growth and consistent change.

What are his secrets? Apart from the above mentioned fear dynamics, he and his leadership are decisive, focused and always aware of the vision and strategy of the organization. They don't let fear distract their focus from executing on their strategic vision and moving forward through change. As a result of this, they do a lot of things right.

Unfounded Fear

While instinctive fear is important and useful, the majority of our fears, worries, and doubts are unfounded, and ultimately unimportant, especially when it comes to the fear of change. However, in the heat and intensity of the moment, these fears and negative forces feel very real – so real that we conclude that they are based on fact, even when they are not. And because we believe that they are real, we not only give them our full attention, taking time and attention away from other more critical issues, we also begin acting on them. Even worse, because they've clouded our perception of the world and the people around us, and therefore altered our "reality," they make us conclude and do things we might not otherwise do.

If we could measure the power and influence of unfounded fear on a scale of zero to ten (with zero being low and ten being high), it should rate a one. However, with unfounded fear, the scale typically rises to an eight or nine for most people, regardless of their rank or position. The problem is that most people are unaware of how far the tentacles of unfounded fear penetrate their thinking. If unfounded fear is at the high level of an eight or nine, then it presents such a large influence that it clouds your vision and your ability to embrace change. Consequently, you get a lot of mis-reads as you attempt to make sound, successful decisions.

Let's say, for example, that you've come up with a business strategy that you believe will be very profitable. The last time you tried a new strategy, though, it didn't work very well, so now you're asking yourself "What if I'm wrong?" and "What if this fails?" Being distracted by this fear of failure, you become hesitant to change and begin holding back instead of moving forward decisively and executing your idea. What happens then? There are two possibilities. First, you don't try it at all, and as a result never reap the benefits the strategy might provide to you, your career, or your company. The second possibility is that you do try, but without the full energy, focus, and passion you would apply if you were confident of success. As a result of this lackluster approach, you are unable to achieve your goal. Either way, the fear has taken its toll. Mediocrity and even failure are the result.

How Fear of Rejection Affects Change

Another unfounded fear that can have a significant effect on individual and team performance is the fear of rejection. Current brain science tells us that the fear of rejection neurologically causes us to experience the same pain as that from a severe physical injury. In other words, when it comes to the pain of rejection, we feel emotional pain in the same way in which we experience physical pain. Is it any wonder then, that the human creature fears rejection? We all work very hard to avoid this pain and now we know why. This has enormous implications on workplace performance.

Here is how the fear of rejection typically works. Let's say, for example, that you're walking into a conference room for an important business meeting. You've never met any of the people in the meeting before, but because you weren't treated as you thought you should have been at the last meeting you attended—or, for that matter, at a meeting you attended ten years ago—you're concerned that you'll be rejected by this group. You become so convinced that they will reject you, that even though they've done *nothing* to make you feel that way, you begin to act defensively. Your defensiveness becomes obvious to those around you, and they respond, understandably, with skeptical caution. You, in turn, sense their caution and apprehension, and conclude that they are, in fact, rejecting you, just as you had suspected they would. And the "fact" that they've rejected you reinforces your negative behavior, which of course gives them more reason to reject you. So before you know it, without realizing what you've done, you've sealed your own fate. Your preoccupation with the fear of rejection has made it a reality. We will look at this fear of rejection in more detail in the next chapter.

How Fear of Failure Affects Change

A third type of unfounded fear is the fear of failure, especially as it relates to money. When business is lean, what's the first thing we usually do? Of course, we cut expenses—normally a sound move. Sometimes, though, because fear clouds our vision—and our thinking—we make poor decisions and cut too much, or cut in the wrong places. How many times have you seen an organization cut sales or marketing expenditures when what they really needed to do was to increase sales?

Similarly, how often do companies cut training/coaching and development expenses in an effort to save money when maintaining such coaching and development expense will reduce turnover, increase productivity, and save them even more? Like other unfounded fears, fear of failure leads us to do things that, if we weren't afraid, we'd never consider doing.

Recognizing fear and its influence is an important first step to becoming a time-effective leader through change. Whether you are allowing some instinctive fear to grow out of balance, or you are being controlled by an unfounded fear, the next chapter discusses how the fear of change (change resistance) can be conquered.

Chapter 6

Conquering Change Resistance

Twenty-five years ago I faced a situation in which fear of change (change resistance) could have negatively influenced the outcome. Working for one of the largest organizations in its field, I (and the other employees) felt a heightened significance and worth just by being part of such an industry leader.

Behind closed doors, however, the leadership of this organization regularly used compromise, deception, and manipulation in order to get their desired result. Daily, I faced the opportunity to join in and be a party to this, just to feel included and not excluded by my peers. This enticement was very real, too. Not only was my job on the line, but also my income, my family's livelihood, reputation, retirement and camaraderie with my peers. The temptation was enormous and real.

But I knew that if I succumbed to the fear of change and compromised my values, I would not be able to live with myself for years to come. Consequently, I knew I had to leave that situation or be consumed, either by my peer's rejection or by my own conscience.

Once I resolved to leave, my situation did not immediately improve. Fear of change, fear of failure, and fear of my family suffering hammered my mind daily. Determined to leave, knowing the ramifications of such a move on me, my family and my career, it still took me another 18 months to muster up the strength to make this life-altering change.

Once I left that organization, things did not get easier. They only worsened. A whole new and different set of concerns and pressures surfaced. I had exchanged one set of pressures for another. The pressure to compromise character was replaced by the pressure of providing for my family and the pressure of my own sense of purpose. The only constants through all of this were *change* and the set of principles that I chose to embrace.

After a year of wrestling with my future, I started the human development organization that I preside over today. In retrospect it was one of the best decisions I ever made. However, during the heat and intensity of the moment, it was anything but pleasant. I now know I made the right decision. In the face of intense fear, doubt and uncertainty, the decision was not easy. But I knew it was the right decision, so I acted on it.

Belief Conquers Fear

You will never conquer fear of change until you believe in yourself, the people around you and your strategy enough to no longer fear the consequences of defying the fear or the change. I will repeat this statement because it is key:

You will never conquer fear until you believe in yourself, the people around you and your strategy enough to no longer fear the consequences of defying the fear of the change.

What does this mean?

It means you must believe in yourself enough to do or say what you know to be right or best, even at the risk or threat of loss or failure. You must learn to embrace change rather than be controlled or consumed by the fear of change. Those who learn to believe in themselves are the ones who possess the right performance skills and time-effective tools to effectively do their jobs and lead through change

If you are a fear-based manager or leader, this is a scary proposition. Why? Because it is the people - not the leadership - that have the ultimate control over the end result. They drive your business and determine its degree of success or failure. As such, they possess the real power and influence. However, many of them simply do not know this, but their *leaders do*.

So, what does the fear-based leader do? As we discussed in Chapter 2, he tries to control through manipulation, coercion or fear tactics. These tools often produce results, but they work only temporarily. Never do they achieve the fullest capacity or potential out of their people. Fear-based tools are counterfeits to authentic leadership ability. They are the trademark tools of a weak individual.

Instead, leadership through change is about personal and internal control, *not* the external control of the people around you. This type of leadership through change is about the control of the *internal* dynamics that drive you and your organization: the feelings, beliefs, thoughts, attitudes, fears and habits that shape your collective behavior and your performance. Ultimately, these internal dynamics drive the external choices, behavior and performance of an individual and an entire team.

What You Fear, Will Happen

When you focus on a particular fear, you often help bring about the very thing that you feared would happen. For example, the thought of failure rivets your focus on the fear of failure itself. You doubt the success of your decision or endeavor. This then causes you to set up a string of bad decisions, out of self-preservation against the fear, that actually create and ensure failure.

How does this happen? When you focus on a fear, you become preoccupied with that fear. When you are preoccupied with a fear you begin doing, saying and thinking things that are more influenced by the fear, rather than by facts or substance. This dynamic works within all of us. Here is an example based on the fear of rejection:

I fear that I will be rejected as I enter a room and interact with a group of people.

⇩

I then become preoccupied with the fear of being rejected.

⇩

At this point, being so preoccupied (mentally and emotionally) with the fear of being rejected, I take on a peculiar behavior while around those in the group.

⇩

My odd behavior becomes obvious to all.

⇩

They respond with skeptical caution.

⇩

As I sense their caution, I feel their apprehension.

⇩

I conclude that they are, in fact, rejecting me, just as I
suspected they would.

⇩

Then, I react with another deliberate, negative, more rejecting behavior while I conclude within myself that they
did as I suspected. They rejected me.

⇩

Before I know it, without realizing it I have sealed my
own fate. My preoccupation with my own fear brought
the fear upon me

Do you see how this happens? It happens to all of us in every area
of our lives   in business, in relationships – everything!

Tree Analogy

One of the most fascinating things I have discovered in my work
with people over the years is that emotions, behavior and habit development can be compared to a tree. With a tree, growth and produc-
tion begins with the root, then progresses through the trunk, out to the
branches and ultimately results in fruit. In order for the tree to produce
different fruit, the changes must begin at the root of the tree.

The same can be said of human behavior and habits. Our emotions go through several stages or progressions before they reveal
themselves through outward, external behaviors (fruits). Our history
(social conditioning) of emotions and fears form the root, and serve
to shape the development of our self-concept and habits. Our habits
in turn, branch out into our attitudes, which ultimately determine our
performance and behavior, or the "fruit" of our lives.

The dynamics of a group or organization can also be better understood through our tree analogy. The root or core behind the personal-

ity, success, and survival of a group is the combination of each individual's emotional, fear, and social history. Therefore, the emotions, habits, and attitudes of each person in the organization are vital to its overall success.

Often we focus on changing the end result or fruit of a company, situation, problem, or even a person, rather than focusing on the root of the problem. That's like cutting off a rotten apple expecting a good apple to grow back in its place. When in fact what we need to do in order to consistently harvest good fruit is to treat the root of the tree. This is why most attempts at change in human performance and behavior fail or are temporary at best. All genuine change, whether within an organization, a person, a department or a system must begin at the root.

Conquering the fear of change and creating time-effective change leadership system-wide begins with each individual in the organization. Conquering fear within an individual is accomplished by learning and applying an appropriate set of tools and strategies for understanding and dealing with the fears and emotions that lie at the root of one's habits, attitudes, and performance.

Any successful approach to creating leadership through change must focus on both an organizational level as well as an individual level, if there is to be genuine, permanent change and growth. *Change then rests upon your ability and your leaders' ability to empower, mobilize and direct the human performance potential within each of your people.* This ability drives and ultimately determines a company's success and future.

How do you acquire the skills that develop the inner strengths needed to conquer one's fear of change, perform time-effectively, stay true to one's principles and, consequently, realize your potential? The chapters in Part II and Part III of this book answer this question.

First, Part II explores the idea that in order to conquer fear's influence, we must know what fear is and how it works.

1. Fear is an emotion.
2. Emotions create habits.
3. Habits can change.
4. Effective performance training-over-time changes habits.

Part III presents a set of practical tools for changing the human behavioral habits (mental, physical, and verbal) that stem from fear.

PART TWO

Chapter 7

Fear Is An Emotion

Water is an incredible resource. Without it, there would be no life on earth. We are totally dependent on water for our survival. Yet, water also has the power to alter and even destroy. Water can physically change nature and human civilization. The enormity and power of water generated attention in March of 2011. That year the great Tohoku, Japan Tsunami struck with a vengeance. Triggered by a 9.0 magnitude undersea mega-thrust earthquake, this tsunami obliterated whole towns and villages. Its powerful waves rose to over 124 feet and traveled as far as six miles inland. Nothing and no one who stood in the path of that tsunami had a chance. Sadly, over 31,000 people were either dead, injured or missing a full two months after the disaster.

It was one of the worse tsunamis to hit the Japanese coast in over 300 years, only surpassed by the Japanese tsunamis of 1707 and 1498!

This tsunami engulfed man-made levies that had stood for decades. As towns and communities were engulfed and obliterated by its mighty power, no one could do anything except attempt to escape. Everyone had to wait on the water. Eventually, the waters receded. However, life did not return to normal for thousands of people. There was no more "normal." "Normal" was swept away by the power and might of the water. From the tsunami of 2011 we learned that sometimes not even man's best engineering devices can dictate or direct the path and power of a channel of water.

The Greatest Power Within You

Emotions work in a similar way to water. Emotions are a powerful force. The power unleashed by our emotions can influence and control what we do, say, think and feel. You know this is true when you think about it. The body cannot consistently dictate or control the rest of our being. Nor can the mind. However, emotions *regularly* do control, dictate and influence our being. Emotions are powerful enough to make us do (through the body), say (through the mouth) and think (through the mind) things that sometimes are not what we want or intend. Emotions can produce behaviors that we disdain, yet feel powerless to change. Emotions can make us feel up (happy, excited) or down (hopeless, frustrated).

Many people are often afraid or unsure of the unbridled power and influence that their emotions can have on their behavior and disposition. This is why we often avoid change, because *the process of change (with its uncertain future and its unknown consequences) can trigger waves of emotion.* And those emotions are sometimes as powerful as an emotional tsunami. For many of us that is scary because:

    a.   we feel we can't control the tsunami of our emotions, and

    b.   who wants to have to feel those feelings anyway?

Consequently, we often will work hard to avoid and resist change in order to avoid the emotions.

Why do we do this? Because we do not *understand* emotions and how they function. This is a fear. It can be a fear of not being in control emotionally or behaviorally, or mabe fear of the unknown.

Emotions appear to be abstract and complex. In reality, however, emotions such as fear are logical and structured. The problem lies in knowing how emotions work. Once we know how they work, we then can see their order, their patterns. We can then begin to see the *logic* behind how emotions operate within human behavior.

Several years ago, one of my clients was the chief executive of a multimillion dollar media empire. He worked feverishly from deal to deal. He always seemed detached and distant with his people (and his family). He was rarely accessible to those who mattered most, his immediate team.

To outsiders he was warm and friendly. But to the rank and file within the organization, his every move was watched. Why? Because he had an explosive, finger-pointing, blame-oriented personality. He was short on praise and quick to blame those around him. He was controlled by his emotions.

How can a company survive under such irrational behavior at the top? In one simple word; money and lots of it. Because this media executive was crafty with his clients, he was highly skilled when it came to deal-making. He knew how to work a customer. He was smooth, relaxed, and confident in those settings.

However, when it came to interacting with those closest to him, he was a disaster. He was irrational, explosive and unpredictable. How can a person exhibit two extremely different temperaments? Is this leadership style rare? Hardly. It is an all-too-familiar style that is tolerated in business, especially when times are financially productive.

The sad thing is that this executive was not happy. He had no peace. He was not content. Although he was accomplished on the outside, he didn't *feel* accomplished on the inside. His life was characterized by stress, tension and isolation.

However, because he held so much power within the organization and because his deal-making made so much money for the company, his behavior was tolerated. Because of this, he was led to believe that his ways were acceptable to those around him because they accepted it. Consequently, he was closed to suggestions that contradicted this belief.

What motivation did he have to change?

What motivation did he have to look within?

What incentive was there to improve his ways?

As long as he kept the machine running and financially productive, and as long as he could continue to hire new people to replace the ones he ran off, he had very little reason to change.

This leadership style destroys the culture of an organization. Work becomes an obligation or duty for the people in the company. Eventually, most only work there for the money. Desire and motivation evaporate. As soon as a better job opportunity comes along, the healthy and emotionally strong people (often the best people) depart. However, those who have the most to risk for leaving will remain and endure, further dismantling their self-esteem and self-confidence.

Was this executive exhibiting a learned behavior, or was he simply made this way? Like all habits, this brute's baggage was learned behavior that developed within him *over time*.

How do emotions work within people like this media executive? Emotions are governed by three truths:

1. Emotions *can* be controlled and re-directed, but you *cannot* eliminate them.
2. Emotions are *reactive*, not proactive.
3. Taking responsibility and ownership, versus blaming and making excuses, is the first step toward emotional self-control.

Emotions Can be Controlled

You *cannot* eliminate fear, the fear of change, or other emotions, but you *can* control and re-direct them.

As with water, the dynamics that make up emotions are powerful. But also like water, emotions can be harnessed, channeled, re-directed and therefore, controlled. With the right tools and strategies you can develop the skills to control negative emotions and gain desired outcome or benefit for yourself, or your team, or your entire organization. The more you learn, know and understand about emotions the easier it is to harness, control and re-direct them.

Emotions React

Emotions are reactive, not proactive. What does this mean? It means that our emotions don't lead or initiate, they follow. Emotions are activated by particular stimuli, or triggers, both positive and negative. Of course, many things can trigger emotions, but they all fall into three general categories: things seen, things thought, and things heard.

For example, let's say that you're at a football game and your team is down by two points. It's first and ten and they're on their own 35 yard line, but there are only 20 seconds left in regulation play. You and all the other fans are on your feet, and begin cheering as soon as the quarterback passes to a tight end near the sideline. As you continue cheering, he catches it and runs across midfield to the 40 before stepping out of bounds. It's first and ten again, but now there are only ten seconds left. The team lines up again, and the quarterback throws a screen that brings them close to the 35. But it's short of a first down, and the receiver can't get out of bounds. Now you're jumping up and down, screaming. Your voice is starting to go hoarse. The kicking team runs out onto the field and lines up. The center snaps the ball and you hold your breath as it sails through the air, passing between the uprights just as the gun sounds. Without even thinking about it, you wrap your arms around the stranger beside you and you both jump up and down shouting with joy.

What's happened, of course, is that you've *reacted* to what you've *seen*–your team marching down the field, what you've *thought*–the team coming closer to winning, and what you've *heard*–your voice, and those of all the other fans, cheering them on. And as they got closer and closer to the goal, your emotions became intensified, heightened, to the point of taking over, albeit in a positive way.

There's also, however, a negative side to all this. Think, for example, about the last time you saw two people having an argument, or were involved in one yourself. Maybe you got home late from work one day because you had a minor accident and dented the car a bit. You might have been only mildly upset, but your spouse started complaining about the fact that you were home late, which made you a little angry. And when you tried to explain why you were late, your spouse cut you off saying he or she didn't have time for excuses because someone had to get dinner ready, which made you a little angrier still. And before you knew it, you were screaming at each other over something that wasn't particularly important in the first place. Again, you were reacting to what you saw–the dent in the car, what you thought–that your spouse wasn't being sensitive to your feelings, and what you heard–your voice, and your spouse's, getting louder and angrier. Emotions are *reactive*.

Take Ownership and Responsibility

If asked, most people will readily say they take ownership for themselves. However, the opposite often proves true when their reactions are observed. If we react to pressure or pain by blaming and pointing fingers, we are not taking ownership. Our *reactions* reveal how we each approach life, relationships and business.

So the question is, when something does *not* go the way you plan or anticipate, how do you react? Do you blame, find fault, or get explosively angry? Do you run, retreat and feel helpless and hopeless? Interestingly enough, both of these reactions are often rooted in fear.

In order to channel and control emotions, we first must accept ownership of those feelings and fears. Blaming others or ignoring negative feelings only keeps us further from positive self-control. Blaming and ignoring also leaves you feeling even more powerless over the situation that triggered the bad emotions or fears in the first place. Why? Because blaming forces you to be dependent upon the performance of others (those whom you've blamed), which only intensifies the feelings of powerlessness, or of being controlled and therefore, out of control.

Personal strength, confidence and courage only come when we force ourselves to plow through the challenges and fears we face in daily life.

It is important to remember that fear is controllable, because it is an emotion. Emotions can be controlled, once we understand how they work. The primary reason emotions can be controlled is because they are habit forming. The next chapter describes how our emotions create those habits.

Chapter 8

Emotions Create Habits

Two of the greatest forces within human behavior are emotions and habits. They shape our personality and behavior. Combined, emotions and habits affect our daily performance subsequently, largely determining our level of success in life, relationships, and business. Because of their repetitiveness, emotions are habit-forming. However, *habits can be changed*, once you know *how* they function. Everyone has habits in four areas:
1. Mental thought patterns
2. Audible habit patterns
3. Physical habit patterns
4. Emotions and feelings

Habits are created through repetition over time. Most habits are not formed after just one happening or occurrence. Habit formation develops when repetition intersects a specific time frame. In other words, when we do, say, think or feel something several times within a given time frame – be it five hours, five days, five weeks or five months – the end result is usually the creation of a new habit, such as a mindset, an action, a verbal reaction or a feeling.

Let's look briefly at each of these four habit areas.

Mental Thought Patterns

When it comes to mental and attitudinal habits, people usually possess one of two types: negative or positive. Negative mental habits include critical thoughts and skepticism. Positive mental habits are hopeful and optimistic.

Most of your thought patterns and attitudes come from one of these two groups, depending on which category you fit in. Once you repeat any thought or hold any attitude approximately a dozen times over the course of three weeks to seven months, it will develop into a habit.

Audible Habit Patterns

The words you repeatedly speak and tones you use when speaking make up your audible habit patterns. Have you ever known someone who was quick to lash out with words that cut like a knife? That is an audible reaction, or a habit pattern. Conversely, have you ever known someone who always responded with praise? That, too, is an audible habit pattern.

Physical Habit Patterns

Physical patterns are the things you do, especially when your mind is *not* engaged. This includes activities like driving to work or home by the same route, or brushing your teeth first thing in the morning. How many times have you left home going in the wrong direction? This is easy to do if the route to your store or friend's house is different from the route you normally take to work.

To capture an awareness of this habit power within you, spend one day noticing how many physical habits you activate without cognitively, consciously deciding to do them. You will be surprised.

Emotions and Feelings

Do you ever find yourself feeling the same feeling at different times and in different places? For example, during the holiday season, depending on whether your overall childhood experiences were good or bad, positive or negative, those same emotional dispositions from your childhood will resurface when you return to the places of your youth. This same childhood state of being will also resurface when in similar, but not necessarily the same circumstances and places as before. That is because that particular emotion is a habit.

This is also why songs can so easily trigger the same emotions (either positive or negative) year after year within us when we hear an "oldie" song from our youth. Emotions create habits.

What about people who struggle with fear and specifically, the fear of change? They have allowed their repeated feelings of fear to become a habit.

Fear Creates Habits of Impatience, Impetuousness, Self-centeredness, Rejection

A senior partner with a Fortune 500 firm faces a constant cycle of frustration.

She is a project-oriented individual, who loves to please her superiors. She's good at what she does. However, she is easily bored and insecure. Since she is always in need of constant affirmation, her superiors sometimes see her as high-maintenance. But because she produces so much business, her "quirk," as they see it, is overlooked.

The frustration is her own. Her emotions drive her to accomplish and achieve on one hand, and appease and please superiors on the other hand. This back-and-forth cycle is weary and exhausting. This habit pattern, rooted in a fear of rejection, seems unstoppable:

Subtle fear of rejection and of being rejected leads to—

⇩

Constant need for acceptance and recognition, which leads

to—

⇩

Disposition and assumptions, which leads to—

⇩

Continually trying to prove self to others, which then leads

to—

⇩

Feel good about self when accomplished or achieved, which

leads to—

⇩

Must always be moving/working to calm the fear, culminat-

ing in—

⇩

Fearful and insecure during slow time or inactivity

Do you see how this happens? It begins with the emotion of fear and slowly progresses until it reveals itself as behaviors for all to see. On the surface, it looks like the typical signs of a workaholic, doesn't it?

To change a person's habit system, you first must uncover the emotion that is at the heart or *root* of what is driving the habit behavior needing to be replaced. Once this is discovered, you can then make changes, because changes always begin at the root. Otherwise, you will spend many fruitless hours, days, weeks, months, and years addressing and dealing with external factors and behaviors that are not at the root of the problem. Consequently, real change never materializes.

So, what emotion is at the root of this woman's insecurity? Fear; fear of inadequacy, fear of failure and fear of rejection.

She is in an endless cycle that imprisons her and she knows it. Over time, this cycle becomes an unbearable burden. Why? Because she needs new challenges, new projects or new clients every 6 to 12 months. She actually is thriving on a form of change. However, it is a change of environment, tasks, and people in order to feed impulse gratification and avoid deep relationships, neither of which are very healthy. This consequent pattern leaves residue in her wake (a topic of discussion for another time). All of this put together, creates problems for her firm. The company's success depends on establishing, building and maintaining client relationships for years, not months.

This cycle creates additional problems for her as well. She is unable to maintain long-term relationships because each new encounter is a short-term "project." At best, this offends those in contact with her. She is also intensely lonely. Why? Because others are put off by her "project" mentality. Also, because she is always so focused on her "projects", she never slows down enough to engage in meaningful interaction, communication and friendship, unless it is with one of her customers. When she is with a customer, she views listening and engaging as parts of her job and she does that well.

While addressing this particular problem one day, she blatantly stated, "I don't want to engage people in conversations when I'm not at work. I do that every day at my job because I have to!"

Being project-oriented creates isolation and loneliness. Desiring the human connection and contact, she struggles with being alone and alienated. Some internal hidden force leads her to be isolated and alone. That force is the emotion of fear.

Many leaders get themselves into this position. They fear intimate, one-on-one interaction on a personal level. They convince themselves that their apprehension is normal. But it's not. However, when you are at the top of your game and you are producing effectively, who's going to call you on it? No one.

This "Lone Ranger Danger," though practiced out of self-preservation and fear, often results in cultural coldness for those around and under the leader as they struggle with feeling rejected or insignificant. The leader's self-distancing habits communicate rejection and superiority.

How does this fear expose itself? In various ways. With our executive, she voices a willingness to serve and help toward those around her. However, when it comes to actually helping another person move forward or get to that next level, she cannot do it for fear of being surpassed or replaced.

As long as others remain under or lateral to her perception of success and accomplishment, she can help them. However, when her own place, position or status, whether real or imagined, is threatened, she finds herself backing away - not supporting, but rejecting; not answering the phone, but distancing herself from the individual seeking her aid or support.

To the other individuals seeking her aid, this comes across as rejection. Subsequently, all who have sought our friend's help have eventually distanced themselves. Inevitably, our executive often finds herself alone.

Consequently, she secures her own place in the social pecking order while rejecting and alienating innocent friends and peers in the process. These behaviors are all motivated by fear, fear of change.

Now I ask you, which is the best use of time, energy and resources in this situation – to work at changing issues of impatience, self-centeredness and loneliness, the surface issues, or to work at conquering fear (of inadequacy, failure and change), the root issue?

Of course, the answer is to conquer the fear. If you conquer and replace the fear with healthy, productive behaviors and attitudes, then all of the surface problems either go away or take care of themselves.

Remember, fear is an emotion. Emotions create habits. Habits *can* change. We'll find out how we can change emotional habits in the next chapter.

Chapter 9

Habits Can Change

Why do things seem to flow easy for some and hard for others? The secret is in their *attitudes*, which ultimately determine performance.

A senior VP of marketing is hampered with self-sabotaging habits. No matter what she does, nothing ever works well. She is never ahead and always behind. She lives and functions from crisis to crisis.

Projects are always late. In short, this senior marketing executive is on overload. Every duty or task is a major undertaking. Though sometimes simple, her tasks often seem arduous.

What's more, she is highly critical and negative of others, both at work and at home. Always frustrated, she's never satisfied. Consequently, she is rarely pleased with herself or her subordinates; many of whom fear her and are convinced they can never do anything right, believing she is waiting for an excuse to terminate each of them.

Performance is directly tied to attitude. Attitudes are simply mental thought patterns, or habits. So, the objective for change should be to identify the underlying attitudes, both the ones that are hindering and holding her back as well as the attitudes which promote peak performance.

This executive's dominant attitude is negative and critical. She sees everything and everyone, including herself and her subordinates, through a negative lense (which interestingly enough is rooted in the emotion of fear). Because of this she is extremely short with those directly under her. She emits negative, critical, skeptical comments regularly. People avoid contact and conversation with her. Consequently, crucial decisions are left incomplete, or at best, delayed.

The Development of Bad Habits
As we begin our work with this executive, we quickly learn several facts.

First, she has a childhood diagnosis of ADD (Attention Deficit Disorder). Second, she failed a grade, further compounding her belief that she is defective or even retarded. Third, her father was hard to please. Consequently, this senior marketing executive felt and feared that she never measured up to her dad's expectations.

How does this personal history influence this senior executive today? Her history shaped her self-concept, which in turn developed her habits. Her habits create her attitudes, and her attitudes determine her personal productivity and effectiveness as she interacts with others.

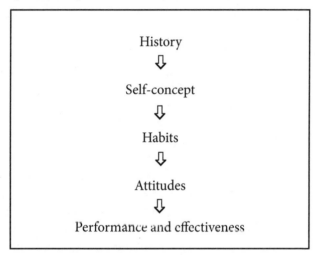

For this executive, the progression goes something like this:

History:
1. As a child, she had a *fear* of rejection, failure and inferiority.
    a. her dad rarely praised her achievements, always accented her short-comings and chose to yell at her instead of creating and enforcing healthy boundaries in her life,
    b. she failed a grade in school, and
    c. the adult experts (professional counselors) diagnosed her with ADD.

Self-concept:
2. Her personal history (above) created the constant drive and need to prove her abilities to herself and to others in order to validate her value and worth.

3. She sets unrealistic goals and objectives which often ensures her failure and further validates her fear about herself of being inadequate.

Habits:

4. Her decisions, which found their genesis in her self-concept, are repeated over time, ultimately transitioning into habits.

5. One of those habits is a constant internal competitiveness – always competing primarily with herself, but also others. She approaches tasks with too short of a time frame, "*I can do this task in one hour*" (when it is clearly a two or three hour job). This is her subconscious attempt to disprove the perception and beliefs she developed from her history (#1 above) and her self-concept (#2 and #3 above). Consequently, she often sets herself up for failure because she rarely completes her jobs within the time frames allotted. Plus, when she repeatedly underestimates her time management and therefore fails to deliver on time, others around her see her as unreliable.

Attitudes:

She is impatient and intolerant, with herself and with others around her, a slave-driver. Why? Because there is an undercurrent of feeling that no matter what she does, it isn't good enough. Her impatience and intolerance are the result or "fruit" of her efforts to dispel the feeling of not measuring up in the first place. Subsequently, she communicates to those working for her that they do not measure up either.

How can we successfully *change* such counterproductive performance in ourselves, others, and whole teams of people? By changing the *habits*.

Habits rule our lives. Habits determine a lot of what we *do*, what we *say*, how we *think* and how we *feel*. If you have good, healthy, positive habits, you'll tend to have positive, healthy thoughts, feelings, attitudes, actions and therefore, performance. The same is true on the negative, critical side as well. If you have negative, critical, skeptical habits you will tend to have less than stellar outcomes with most of your projects, endeavors, or relationships.

So, the issue is in *changing* an individual's habit structure, something that is usually formulated in childhood.

Habits *Can* Change

Is it possible to change the habits of a person, team, department or organization? Yes. However, it takes concentrated effort, the correct tools and strategies, coupled with a training-over-time training/development model.

Bad habits are hard to break. You can't change a habit by focusing on that habit. As a matter of fact, the more you focus on the bad habit the more entrenched the habit becomes within one's behavior and personality. This is why a person will have difficulty with losing weight while dieting. What does a diet, or restriction from food, cause you to think about? Food. So then, how can you break the habit of nibbling when your mind is preoccupied with the very thing you want to change or conquer?

The only way to genuinely and permanently conquer a habit is by *replacing* the old habit with a new one. As you practice the new habit through training-over-time, or through constant, consistent practice of the new activity, the new habit eventually replaces the old one.

How did an Emmitt Smith or a Walter Peyton know where and when to cut downfield? How did a Michael Jordan know when to pull up and shoot the ball?

Or, how did my daughter, Maria (see Introduction), know how to jump up in the air from the service line of a volleyball court and not only hit the ball over to the opponent's side of the court, but cause the ball to immediately drop to the floor to within 10 feet of the net after crossing the net? Or, how was she able to serve the ball with the intention of nailing a targeted defender in the chest, hard, in order to back the defender up further away from the volleyball net just so Maria could then serve the next ball to within 10 feet of the net once the ball had crossed over into the opponents side of the court (both of which feats are extremely difficult to pull off, requiring such precision)?

The first answer we most often hear to these above questions is "instinct."

And what is behind instinct? *Habit formation.* What is behind habit formation? *Repetition* or consistent *training-over-time.* Highly skilled people do *not* attain their level of talent through seminars, lectures or unorganized, unstructured coaching. Norman Brinker, the Father of Casual Dining and founder of such restaurant chains as Steak and Ale, and Chile's, once told me that we create our own luck through our own consistent, hard work. The key word there is "consistent."

So, with the consistent practice of the right thinking, attitudes and actions, Emmitt, Walter, Michael, and my daughter all created their own luck. What were the habits that created the "luck" for each of them? Michael Jordan was always the first individual to arrive at practice and the last man to leave practice. Walter Peyton spent hours running bleachers and hillsides before it was fashionable to do so. Emmitt Smith could always be found working out, building his leg strength and body mass – so much so that on more than one occasion, defensive players remarked that hitting Emmitt Smith was like *being hit* by a rock. Additionally, Maria spent hours every day of every week of every month, for five solid years through junior high and high school serving a volleyball over a net. Consequently, in each instance, habits were formed through continual practice or training-over-time, developing strength and "muscle memory."

This is precisely how Maria grew from failing to make her 8th grade volleyball team to being recruited by Northwestern University of the Big Ten Conference in just five short years. She worked and practiced more, harder and longer than most of her peers over that same period of time. That hard work, over an extended period of time, changed many of Maria's behavioral *habits*. It transformed her into a peak performer mentally and physically. In the process it also transformed her attitude, confidence and disposition. However, her transformation started way back in 8th grade with Maria having to *daily* work at conquering *many* internal fears (most of which have already been introduced in this book); especially the fear of change that once controlled her behavior and daily interaction.

Invariably, excellence in performance comes from out-of-the-ordinary habit formation or training-over-time. This is true for mental, physical, verbal, and emotional habits.

The more times you think a thought, do a deed, speak a word or feel a feeling, the greater the likelihood that it will become a habit. So, choose what you wish to become habit and begin repeating it often.

The following phrase makes habit formation a positive exercise:

Sow a thought, reap a deed,
Sow a deed, reap a habit,
Sow a habit, reap a destiny.

In the next chapter, the concept of performance training-over-time is presented in more detail. Training-over-time is an essential ingredient for changing habits long-term.

Chapter 10

Training-Over-Time Changes Habits

Is there a process or system available today that teaches an individual how to conquer the fear of change, while at the same time producing the right attitudes and thinking behind leadership development and time-effective performance? Is there a training model that sufficiently addresses the fear factor?

Yes. To genuinely address a change in human performance, thinking, and decision-making we have to strike at the core of what drives human performance – our habits. The human creature is a creature of habits. Studies tell us that the vast majority of our habit patterns are developed during the first five years of our lives. In other words, the experiences we encountered over a five year period developed into habits. Those habits then developed our thinking and performance. Now, if it takes five years during the most fertile time of our lives to create and develop a habit, why then do we think we can change that habit in just a few hours (through a lecture or a few coaching sessions) or over a weekend (through a retreat or seminar)?

Common sense reveals the futility of this notion. However, individuals and organizations allocate and spend billions of dollars annually on processes that time and again prove themselves to be at best, less than effective.

Like the computer software industry of twenty-five years ago, the industry of human development is highly fragmented today. That is why fear of change, as it relates to human performance, continues to exist unabated and unaddressed.

Seminars, books and even experts espouse what to do and how to think. However, what is needed is a universal, systematic training standard that is reliable, effective and affordable. We need a standard that has broad-based application potential, one that can be deployed throughout an organization, regardless of channels or layers.

Reliable, Time-Effective Training

By the very nature of the problem, several features are required of this standard:

1. Practical *tools and strategies* that afford the trainee the ability to develop skills to affect the intangible (weak or wrong attitudes, habits, or thinking which developed out of fear or other negative emotions), with a tangible (time-effective tools).

2. A tailored *plan or roadmap* of performance training/coaching and leadership development that has a definite beginning and end. Such training/coaching should include time-effective tools that develop the inner strengths of:

    a. *self-control* over fear and other emotions,

    b. ability to *focus* without distractions, and

    c. *vision* development.

3. *Training-over-time.* Habit formation requires training-over-time with the right tools. One-day functions, weekend retreats, and motivational -- informational seminars all have their place. However, they have not, do not, and will not produce a change in behavioral performance required by today's competitive economic environment. A study by Case Western Reserve University's Weatherhead School of Management found that corporate America lavishes $10 billion *per year* on leadership training. In addition, their studies showed that the benefits of seminar-centered schooling (i.e., lectures, classes, workshops) vanish *within months*, while the impact of one-on-one training and coaching lasts up to *seven (7) years*! Short-term training options can and do produce short-term motivation, renewed hope or purpose. However, for genuine, long-term behavioral performance change, we need a training-over-time model that helps us replace our old habits with new ones.

The Right Tools and Strategies, Coupled with Training-Over-Time, Affect Change

The right tools and strategies, coupled with training-over-time, produce and develop our *habit system*. Our habit system then determines our *personality*. Our personality produces or determines our *behavior*. Our behavior determines our *approach and outlook* with people, work and life. Our approach and outlook determine our *performance*. Our performance determines our degree of *success and accomplishment* throughout life's journey.

On a chart, it looks something like this:

Effective tools and a training-over-time model
Produce

Our habit system, which
Determines

Our personality, which
Produces

Our behavior, which
Determines

Our approach and outlook with people, work and life
Determines

Our performance, which
Determines

Our degree of success and accomplishment throughout life's journey

Successful People Know The Secret

Throughout history great people have learned to master the negative fear of change and forces that disqualify or distract others. They have done this by developing the internal, time-effective skills that keep them focused on their vision and aligned with their values and principles. Time-and-again these people have been characterized by the inner strengths of self-control, focus and vision.

If we are going to invest in ourselves or our people, we should invest in human performance technology that produces the greatest return on investment, that which produces the time-effective performance most needed. We should invest in human performance technology that by its fundamental nature has a greater likelihood of succeeding, and therefore increases the value of your human capital. We should invest in training that reduces costs, increases productivity and grow revenues. With the desired result in mind, *we should invest in Training-over-Time.*

Michael Jordan

Undoubtedly, Michael Jordan is one of the greatest athletes of all time. Many believe he is single-handedly responsible for making professional basketball as popular as our national pastime and the professional gridiron.

It never ceases to thrill me when I discover the underlying reasons for greatness in a person or organization. With Michael Jordan, as is so often the case, both his work ethic and his approach to fear contributed to his success.

Like most highly successful athletes, Michael Jordan believes in a training-over-time training model (athletes refer to it as "practice"). He was always the first to arrive and the last to leave when it came to basketball practice (a common characteristic of top athletes). While others would take practice lightly, Jordan would work with the intensity of a playoff game. This fact often created tension with his teammates who were less inclined to exert a full effort during practice.

What made Michael Jordan one of the greatest athletes of the twentieth century? What made him an incredibly valuable commodity? The answer is his talent, skill and ability. How did his talent, skill and ability develop? Through his training habits *and* his attitude toward fear.

Listen to Jordan's approach to fear and his attitude toward work.

*"I never looked at the consequences of missing a big shot. Why? Because when you think about the consequences, you always think of a negative result. Some people get frozen by that **fear of failure**. They get it from peers or from just thinking about the possibility of a negative result. They might be afraid of looking bad or being embarrassed.*

I realized if I was going to achieve anything in life, I had to be aggressive. I had to get out there and go for it. I don't believe you can achieve anything by being passive. I'm not thinking about anything except what I'm trying to accomplish.

Any fear is an illusion. You think something is standing in your way, but nothing is really there. What's there is an opportunity to do your best and gain some success. If it turns out my best isn't good enough, then at least I'll never be able to look back and say I was too afraid to try. Failure always made me try harder the next time.

I think fear sometimes comes from a lack of focus or concentration. If I stood at the free-throw line and thought about 10 million people watching me on the other side of the camera lens, I couldn't have made anything. So, I mentally tried to put myself in a familiar place. I thought about all those times I shot free throws in practice and went through the same motion, the same technique that I had used thousands of times. Doing this allows you to forget about the outcome.

I approach practices the same way I approach games. You can't turn it on and off like a faucet. I couldn't dog it during practice and then, when I needed that extra push late in the game, expect it to be there. But that's how a lot of people approach things.

And that's why a lot of people fail. They sound like they're committed to being the best they can be. They say all the right things; make all the right moves and motions. But when it comes right down to it, they're looking for reasons or excuses, instead of answers and solutions.

If you are trying to achieve, there will be roadblocks. I've had them; everybody has them."

I Can't Accept Not Trying, Michael Jordan
How to Be Like Mike, Pat Wiliams with Michael Weinreb

Through training-over-time (practice), Michael Jordan developed habits that embraced the factors of fear and led to great success.

Training-Over-Time Affects Productivity

According to the Harvard Business Review, one in three high-potentials admit to not working at their full capability. Our experience supports these claims.

If we use this first figure alone, then does that mean that if your company generated $600 million last year, then there is a realistic expectation that you *lost* $200 million due to inefficient time usage (both physical *and* mental time), poor communication, and work skills that, at the source, exist because of some influences of fear, especially the fear of change? And if your organization produced $12 billion last year, does that then mean that you lost $4 billion in inefficiency and low productivity due to fear? If your team or department was responsible for a third of your company's revenues last year, does that then mean that there is a decent likelihood that you *missed out* on an additional one third of revenue? It is sobering to reflect on the ramifications isn't it?

If you were able to capture and/or generate that additional revenue that was lost on an annualized basis, how valuable would you become to your organization? The right human performance technologies, which include the correct time-effective tools and strategies, recaptures a lot of lost productivity, which translates into dollars on the bottom line at the end of the day. And the capital outlay for time-effective training-over-time is far less than most organizations *waste* each year on unproductive training, coaching and seminars.

In the next chapter, we look at more examples of how a training-over-time approach replaces old habits with new ones and improves overall time-effective performance in individuals and organizations. We also explore the three major areas where effective human performance training is needed in businesses today.

Chapter 11

Changing Habits Can Improve Performance

Top professional athletes are to the sports industry what top leadership talent is to global business: rare and expensive. The war for global business talent is real. The company that recruits, retains and trains the best and the most, wins.

Long ago, I read a Wall Street Journal article that voiced the sentiments of many. The article was titled, *"What Happens When Your Valued Employee Makes a Bad Manager?"* In this article, three executives were asked for their expert opinions on dealing with bad managers. All three sounded knowledgeable. However, with the exception of firing and replacing the bad manager, not one of the interviewees gave a solid solution to the problem. *No one* offered a solution that would help or change the person behind the management problem.

The world is full of people who can tell us *what* the problem is. Through testing, we can detect *who* is most likely to possess the problem. However, we are hard pressed to find solutions that show us *how* to eliminate the problem and produce genuine, positive change within our human capital.

Performance training/coaching – specifically, a training-over-time model – coupled with time-effective *tools and strategies* produce a change in performance within individuals, teams and whole organizations. The changes manifest themselves in varied forms: leadership ability, strategic thinking, dramatically improved communication skills, higher morale, changed behavioral habits, increased productivity, and the ability to work with change.

However, the existing talent pool is limiting performance across-the-board because of a lack of know-how in regards to recruiting, retention, personal time-effectiveness, leadership ability, and change resistance. An organization's largest annual capital expenditure (people) consistently restricts its productivity and growth because of change resistance and performance issues. And yet, businesses are facing a dramatic leadership talent shortage. Every organization is vulnerable.

The War For Top Talent Is Real

As in sports, there are three types of "players" in business:

- 1st stringers – employer-minded, ownership and leadership minded, consistently faces and embraces fear of change with proactive energy.
- 2nd stringers – employee-minded, *"Tell me my job and I will do it well,"* looks to superiors and peers to make the first move.
- 3rd stringers – paycheck minded, *"I will put in my 40 hours and that's it,"* expects everyone else to make *all* of the moves.

The war for 1st string, productive talent is upon us. The company that employs the most 1st string talent wins. It is that simple. On a personal level, doing what it takes to function like an owner and a champion (beyond just the technical aptitudes), places you in the best possible position to take advantage of this competition.

Traditional methods of dealing with 2nd and 3rd string players are old, outdated and far too costly. Winning solely by replacing existing talent is expensive and filled with problems and pitfalls, especially when today's mis-hire rates average 50%. This translates into one failure for every successful new-hire experience.

So, how do you win this war for top talent? By being proactive and providing time-effective leadership training and development in three key areas:

- Finding and securing peak performers, thus avoiding the high costs of mis-hires.
- Changing and transforming the existing talent pool (rather than replacing and displacing).
- Retaining/motivating key people once they are on board.

Time-effective training/development permanently changes habits, retains talented, top people and creates highly productive leaders who work through change. As top athletes have learned, the only type of training that accomplishes this task is training-over-time, coupled with time-effective tools and strategies.

The Need for Peak Performers

Through our firm's Executive Survey, we asked current and former senior executives (C-suite to VPs) the following question, *"What is the #1 most pressing problem you face?"*

The number one answer, by a 2 to 1 margin was:

"surrounding myself with qualified people."

Tied for number two were:

"the stress and pressure of delivering on expectations," and
"emotional regulation, self-control."

Understandably, the least problematic issue was *"self-confidence."*

Transforming Existing Talent

What happens when you realize your organization is filled with a lot of 3rd string players, a few 2nd stringers and few, if any, 1st string stars? You're in big trouble. Your organization's days of survival are numbered unless you make some dramatic changes, fast. You need to transform some 2nd and 3rd string players into 1st string performers. This begins by improving most of your players to a higher level of interactive and time-effective performance through an effective training-over-time leadership training and development model.

Let's look at an example of a 2nd string player named Melanie who could be turned into a 1st string player with the right training approach. When asked to send an email to all appropriate parties, Melanie thinks she is carrying out a simple task and proceeds to do just that. However, days later, her supervisor finds out that a couple of key people never received the email announcement. When the supervisor addresses the issue with Melanie, in an attempt to find and remedy the problem, her response is that she does not know how these two never received the announcement as she sent it out to everyone on the list.

When, over the course of six months, this same type of problem occurs at least once a month, the supervisor realizes she has to correct this situation. Traditional thought is to either transfer Melanie out to another role, send her to a training seminar, or terminate her.

However, seminars have been tried before and they've proven ineffective for Melanie. Termination is out of the question as well, since her personality and customer appeal bring the company a value that is hard to find or replace. Melanie is great with customers. Her supervisor understands that Melanie's personality and charm with customers is what keeps some of them coming back for more.

At this point you may say, "Then the easy move is to transfer Melanie over to another department." However, for her supervisor, although this was an option, it was not a good option. Why? Because Melanie's supervisor will simply be transferring her problem onto someone else within the organization. Realizing they must get to the bottom of this dilemma, Melanie's supervisor takes the matter into her own hands.

After an extensive fact-finding interview with Melanie about her engagement of the tasks in question, what Melanie heard, what she thought, what she did, etc., Melanie's supervisor discovers the flaw in Melanie's actions. Melanie was *assuming* that all of the intended recipients of the email announcement were listed together on one of several past emails sent out. What Melanie did not know was that since three different people sent out previous email announcements (all of which Melanie had at her disposal) to this key group of people, all three recipient lists were slightly different from the other two. One name was missing from two of the lists while two other names were missing from another list. Consequently, when Melanie sent out her email announcement, depending on which list Melanie chose to rely on as her "master", Melanie's efforts were doomed for failure before she ever completed the task, no matter how much effort and hard work she put into the job.

As a result of this simple oversight, Melanie cost her company the loss of a $3 million dollar contract with one of those missed recipients for the following year. In addition to that, her actions cost the company another long-standing customer who'd decided to take their business elsewhere after having this communication breakdown occur with them several other times in the past.

All of us make assumptions. The problem is that some of us make assumptions that actually increase the likelihood of success, while others make assumptions that sabotage our efforts. Can you see how Melanie's thinking and approach to a simple task can consume and waste, versus produce good results? Do you see how just one false assumption can lead to gross communication breakdown and failure? Such an approach in thinking and decision-making costs in time, labor, materials, money, and loss of additional business and revenue.

To make matters worse, Melanie's constant oversights and miscues do not end at work. Melanie's mishaps have created more than their fair share of problems for her marriage and family. Melanie has struggled with depression and depressive behavior for much of her adult life, mostly due to perplexity over the inability to fix this problem.

Why has this problem plagued Melanie for so long? It basically boils down to her assumptions and habits, both of which, once discovered, are changeable.

Melanie had a charmed life in childhood. This resulted in two dynamics: one very positive and one not so good. On the positive side, because of her sheltered, nurtured past, Melanie sees everyone and everything through rose-colored glasses. When it comes to customer service and interaction, Melanie is a natural. She's warm, receptive, inviting and caring with the company's customers. Melanie naturally focuses her full attention on each and every customer. Others' attempts at such personable, winsome behavior can come across as less than genuine. But not for Melanie.

On the flip side, because of her emotionally sheltered background, Melanie never developed an *eye toward detail*. She never had to. Melanie always felt unconditional acceptance growing up, regardless of the outcome of her choices. Consequently, she never struggled with having to change or alter her thinking or behavior in order to measure up to gain acceptance and approval.

In actuality an eye to detail often has its genesis in fear. One becomes detail oriented so as not to displease others (typically a parent, teacher, sibling or friend). It is developed as an attempt to avoid rejection or disapproval and therefore, the fear of the same!

The good thing is that Melanie's situation is not hopeless. She can change because her behavior simply consists of the sum total of all of her habits. And as we know, habits can change. With the right tools and strategies, coupled with a focused effort *over time*, Melanie can replace her old habits with new and improved ones.

Retaining and Motivating Your Key People

Because of fear's influence, especially the fear of change, many organizations are depending on 3rd string players when they need 1st string *partners*. Even more, organizations are relying on 2nd and 3rd string managers when they need 1st string *leaders* to survive and succeed.

Is it possible to motivate 3rd stringers into becoming 1st stringers? Yes! How? By *empowering* each person's leadership potential: their

hidden talent, skills, ingenuity, creativity and abilities. This requires
the conquering of time-stealing fear within that individual, which can
be accomplished by applying the performance tools described in Part
III.

PART THREE

Chapter 12

The Tools/Strategies

"The brain has an incredible power to change as a result of learning and practice. However, it takes a lot of time and intensive practice to create those changes. Unless there is a significant reason (job security, ambition to rise to the top, or an external mentor/coach), people are unlikely to change if the change requires a great deal more effort than their old way of doing things.

<u>All new learning involves changes in the brain</u>. Existing neural circuits are progressively modified in the process of learning (and change).

<u>Intensive practice</u> can cause the very structure of the brain to change.
The Brain Advantage, Van Hecke, Callahan, Kolar, and Paller

Editor's Note: Review Chapter 2 before proceeding with the remainder of *Change is Good.*

Coach Vince Lombardi led the Green Bay Packers from 1959 to 1967. During his term as head coach with the Packers he had a winning percentage of .758. Today the National Football League's super bowl trophy bears his name. Undoubtedly, Coach Lombardi was one of the greatest coaches of all-time.

Another great coach, Tom Landry, coached the Dallas Cowboys for 29 years. During his tenure the Cowboys record was 271-180-6, and they won two Super Bowls. Though polar opposites in their style and approach to coaching, both Lombardi and Landry were great winners. Forgotten is the fact that these two great coaches played and worked together (with the New York Giants of the 50's) for six years.

I vividly remember the Ice Bowl NFL championship game between the Green Bay Packers and the Dallas Cowboys in 1967. Frankly, the Packers did not play that great of a game. Weather conditions with a wind chill factor of 70 degrees below zero and an average temperature of 13 degrees had something to do with that, I'm sure. However, Lombardi's teams always seemed to find a way to win. It was in that same spirit that his team, yet again, pulled out a victory, with the last play of the game on a blistering cold day.

Coach Lombardi took a losing team in 1959 and instilled discipline, self-respect and confidence. The results of this coaching model were reflected throughout the 60's as the Green Bay Packers won five championships and two Super Bowls in that decade.

For his final game as coach of the Green Bay Packers, Super Bowl II against the Oakland Raiders in 1968, Lombardi's team won with only *ten plays:* five offensive plays and five defensive plays. That was part of the magic of his system – simplicity. The offense ran the same plays over and over again, regardless of the defensive alignments. Success depended on *execution*, not complexity.

Simplicity and Execution

Success and winning often come through *simplicity* and *execution*. Many people wrongly assume that complexity holds some sort of magical key to success that only a few possess. Nothing could be further from the truth. No matter whether it is a new discovery or a new achievement, simplicity and execution are usually at the core of accomplishment.

Effective tools should not be complex. The power of effective tools and strategies is accomplished with their habitual application through training-over-time. Mental telepathy or osmosis will not change a person's or team's thinking and performance. Successful change depends on the constant and consistent execution of effective, specifically designed tools and strategies applied to daily experiences.

As we have discussed in previous chapters, the training-over-time model of performance development consistently produces successful results because it reinforces the execution or implementation of specific behavioral and attitudinal tools and skills over time. In other words, as both Coach Lombardi and Coach Landry would agree, winning is dependent upon practicing and then executing the right plays or tools.

Effective, long-term performance change for individuals, teams and entire organizations requires repetition, practice and execution of the correct tools and strategies. Training-over-time is the most cost effective training model through which to secure the needed results. Traditional training models such as seminars, lectures and even some forms of coaching, when added together over a two to three year period, fall short of expectations because they lack the two elements required for genuine habit and performance change: training-over-time and substantive tools/strategies to execute the needed changes. In addition to that, the costs of these other underperforming training models, when compared over that same two to three year time frame, far exceeds the total outlay of funds for effective training-over-time development models.

The Skills and Tools

Coach Lombardi's strategy hinged on two fundamental techniques:

1. Training-over-time (consistent practice), which produces consistent execution, and
2. Keeping things simple. Using simple, but effective tools (plays). Five for offense and five for defense.

These two techniques together produce effective, productive teams and leaders.

Over the years, our firm has worked with several thousands of people both on an individual and an organizational basis. Through this experience we've discovered twelve basic dynamics or skills that influence or govern performance (individual and organizational):

- Self-control
- Ownership and responsibility
- Listening skills
- Communication and articulation
- Optimism and hope
- Consistency
- Conquering fear/fear of change
- Teamwork
- Mutual respect
- Attitude
- Boundaries
- Principle-centered conduct

Almost everyone recognizes the skills required for advancement and growth. However, there is a short supply of substantive tools/strategies that not only tell us, but show us *how* to develop and acquire those skills that change and improve attitudes, behavior and performance. The tools/strategies are the instruments of change. When exercised consistently, the tools should develop the internal skills. Developed skills preserve and uphold principles and productive behavior. Principles are the governing undercurrents of life. Tools/strategies are

needed to breathe life into the principles. It is in the application of
the tools that the skills get exercised and activated. When this occurs,
individuals, whole teams and organizations experience genuine performance change.

   Throughout two decades of practical application, our organization has developed over 400 performance tools and strategies. Six of
them are specifically designed to conquer and control the influences
of fear and the fear of change in human performance (which is one of
the twelve basic skills listed above). Taken individually, each tool/
strategy is simple. Each one consists of an activity to do or a question to ponder whenever you feel a fear-based emotion begin to occur. Through the consistent, daily application and execution of these
tools/strategies, using training-over-time, you eliminate the influences
of fear and change resistance in your decision-making and execution
abilities and activate the hidden leadership talent within you and your
team.

- *Change is Good* **Tool/Strategy #1:** *What am I afraid of? Why am I afraid?*
- *Change is Good* **Tool/Strategy #2:** *Be proactive, not reactive.*
- *Change is Good* **Tool/Strategy #3:** *What is the worst that could happen?*
- *Change is Good* **Tool/Strategy #4:** *Make yourself do, say or think the exact opposite.*
- *Change is Good* **Tool/Strategy #5:** *Resist "what if" thinking Ask, So what, who cares, what does it matter?*
- *Change is Good* **Tool/Strategy #6:** *Many are called, but few are chosen. What am I doing today to qualify myself?*

   The chapters ahead explore each of these fearless leadership tools/
strategies in greater detail, and provide some guidelines for applying
each tool to your life. But first, let's look at some general instructions
for implementing each tool on a personal and professional level.

Preparatory Instructions for Using the *Change is Good* Tools
   Do you want to conquer the influences of fear of change or change
resistance? Do you want to be free of hesitation, extreme caution,

paralysis-by-analysis, anxiety, worry and doubt about the decisions faced by you and your team? Then use the steps below to practice the six fearless leadership tools/strategies over the next fourteen days to twelve weeks by choosing either the Short-term or Regular-term time frame.

You may choose one of two time-frames to activate your performance change. Choosing the Short-term model may deliver short-term relief, but with this model long-term and even permanent change will be questionable. We take our clientele through the Regular-term time model simply because our clients expect long-term, consistent results and a format followed over twelve or more weeks better insures long-term results.

Short-term Training Time
  *recite each tool 20-25 times per day, out loud.
  *practice each tool at least 5 times per day.
  *practice each tool for 3 days exclusively before moving on to the next tool.
  *3 days multiplied by 6 tools takes 18 days or two and one half weeks for completion.

Regular-term Training Time
  *recite each tool 20-25 times per day, out loud.
  *practice each tool at least *once* per day.
  *practice each tool for 14 days exclusively before moving on to the next tool.
  *14 days multiplied by 6 tools takes 12 weeks or 3 months for completion.

Begin working with only the first tool for either 3 or 14 days (three for Short-term and 14 for Regular-term training time), then add the second tool for the next 3 or 14 days while continuing to work on the first one. Add a new tool every 3 or 14 days until you are comfortable using all six tools. Doing this allows you to develop new habits that neutralize the negative power, sting and influence that comes with fear of change and change resistance. But you will not see how this system works until you *experience* it working within you. So, execute and exercise each tool precisely as it is prescribed.

To begin using these tools, secure a set of index cards and a small spiral-bound notebook from your local office supply store.

Step # 1. Write each tool on an individual index card. One card per tool. One tool per card. The reason for writing it down is that you then have a visual cue to review the tool throughout the day. You may even want to write each tool down on three index cards – one to carry with you, one to keep on your desk at work, and the third to put on the dashboard of your car or some place at home where you'll see it frequently.

Step # 2. For 3 or 14 days, exercise each tool by reviewing the tool audibly, out-loud, 20 to 25 times each day. You may feel a little silly doing this at first, but it's essential that you say the words out loud rather than just in your head. The most important reason for doing this is that it makes you more alert to, and prepared for, your next encounter with a fear or negative thought. This, in turn, enables you to *react* differently than you have in the past, which is the only way to break an old pattern of behavior and create a new, more productive one.

Step # 3. Put each tool into practice each and every time you have an opportunity to use it – whenever you recognize the feeling of fear in any of its forms (rejection, failure, etc.). You may find yourself exercising a particular tool several times a day, depending on how deeply entrenched that particular fear influence has become in your psyche. If the tool requires a physical action on your part, execute or fulfill that action immediately. If the tool requires you to ponder a question, then pause long enough to think through your answer to the question.

This idea of executing the tool in the face of the fear is the most important step in any process of behavioral modification. How else are you going to change your old habits, your old *reactive* behavior, unless you physically and/or cognitively do something that contradicts the patterns you've already established? If you wish to conquer fear's power over your thinking and performance, but don't use the tools in the "trenches" of your job and life, you're wasting your time. The habits will not change, your thinking will not change, and your performance will not change.

Step # 4. Use your notebook to keep a log of *every* instance in which you exercise the tool, briefly noting the date and time the feeling occurred, what the feeling was, and what triggered the feeling. Use a separate page for each occurrence, as you will be adding some comments at the end of the week.

It is very important that you record your experiences in this way. The log represents another visual reminder to do the exercise. Furthermore, if you want to experience a paradigm shift, a change of habit, or overcome the power that these poor habits have over you, you must *do* something *different*. With these tools and their visual cues constantly reminding you to think, speak, and act differently, you will be able to do so when such behavior is appropriate. The visual aspects of the tools aid you in breaking those detrimental, previously-established patterns of thought, emotions, and behavior. And when you've broken a pattern, even once, you've won half the battle for genuine change.

Step #5. At the end of each week, review all the entries in your written log. As part of the review, you should answer the following questions for each log entry, in writing, in your notebook.
- How did I respond or react to this situation?
- What did I experience (think and/or feel) by using this tool in this situation?
- What did I realize (about life, myself, or others) from using this tool in this situation?
- What did I learn (about myself, my business, other people, etc.) from this experience?

If you ignore the writing aspect of these tools, the impact or change you are expecting may *not* occur. The writing portions of the exercise are crucial to the overall effectiveness.

Doing the above five steps with each tool, one-at-a-time, creates a significant difference with whatever habit or fear you address. It takes *at least* three to sixteen weeks of consistent practice and application for you to notice significant changes in your attitude, behavior and performance. However, most individuals begin noticing a difference within the first seven to fourteen days.

So after you have practiced these tools for the initial 14-day period, commit to an additional 14 days. Repeat this commitment *every 14 days* until your reactive behavior has changed and your fear of change is harnessed. Once *your reactions* to events, circumstances and/or people *change* from fear to decisiveness, confidence and peace, then you know that you are successfully executing on the tools. Until then, the tool exercise is not complete. So stay with it. Don't let up. Don't give up until you win, until you experience *change*. If it is taking longer than you'd anticipated, then the question often is, "who is going to win, you or the influences of fear and the resistance to change?" It is totally up to you!

Chapter 13

Deja vu All Over Again!

Tool/Strategy #1: What Am I Afraid Of?
Why Am I Afraid?

Not too long ago, progress was at an all-time high. Technology promised rapidly rising living standards, expanding markets, and increasing consumer growth. Unemployment was at an all time low. It seemed as if everyone was "playing the market." Consumerism ruled the economy. Everyone was happy. Money was plentiful. Twelve-month, no payments, no interest financing was readily available for almost every conceivable product from cars to consumer electronics.

However, just three years later, things changed. At first, the change was slight and incremental. The experts originally termed it a slow-down from the robust economy. It was triggered by a tremendous sell-off in stocks. Institutional investors lost billions. Common people lost their life savings. Fortunes vanished overnight.

There was an initial steep sell-off in the stock market. Prices did seem to bounce back, though not to their original point. Consequently, the country seemed to be getting by. At least that was what everyone wanted to believe. We wanted to believe that it was just a slow-down. However, as month after month passed by, it became obvious that things were not returning to their former glory. The stock market slowly declined to *one tenth* of what it was at its peak just three years before. Bankruptcies steadily grew. With increased bankruptcies and business failures popping up like fields of wheat, banks closed their doors in insolvency.

Experts no longer said this was a slowdown. They termed it a recession. Retail prices fell by more than 10% per year during the three year period. Residential real estate lost one third of its value across the board.

Unemployment ballooned up to 25%. Unemployed workers rioted from one end of the continent to the other. Crime experienced an upsurge over these three years as well.

Globally, we experienced an unprecedented worldwide peace. For the first time in recorded history, no nation was at war with another. However, world economies were anything but peaceful. People everywhere were scared. From Europe to Asia, economies teetered on the brink of collapse. Some went bankrupt. At home, fear and worry ruled the mindsets of everyone, including businesses, government workers, and Middle America. It was not a matter of putting off purchases; there simply was no money to purchase anything.

Looking for someone to blame, the nation pointed their collective finger at the President of the United States. From America's eye, it seemed as if the President sat idly in the comfort and safety of the White House during the previous three years, almost as if he were a spectator at a sporting event, while the entire nation was being slaughtered by the lions. However, this was no sporting event. In reality, the presidential leadership was too passive during this three year decline, probably due to the fear of making a wrong decision. People everywhere were frightened and weary. The future did not look promising.

Within this backdrop, a new President was ushered in. On the day of his inauguration, he told the Nation:

> *"I am certain my fellow Americans expect that on my induction into the Presidency I will address them with a candor and a decision which the present situation of our Nation impels.*
>
> *This is pre-eminently the time to speak the truth, the whole truth, frankly and boldly. Nor need we shrink from honestly facing conditions in our country today. This great Nation will endure as it has endured, will revive and will prosper.*
>
> *So, first of all, let me assert my firm belief that* **the only thing we have to fear is fear itself**—*nameless, unreasoning, unjustified terror which paralyzes needed efforts to convert retreat into advance. . . "*

"The Only Thing We Have to Fear is Fear Itself"

Although this story sounds earily like today's world environment in 2012, it is not. Franklin D. Roosevelt spoke these fateful words on March 4, 1933. He exposed fear for what it is, an inanimate object of sometimes gargantuan proportions. You cannot see, hear or touch fear. However, you can definitely *feel* fear. President Roosevelt spoke about fear as if it were a living organism. Though it had no life of its own, this emotion was responsible for buckling our nation's citizenry to their knees. The President referred to this fear as *"nameless, unreasoning, unjustified terror which paralyzes needed efforts to convert retreat into advance."*

If we are to conquer fear and fear of change, or at the very least remove its power and impact over our thinking and decisions, we must rely on a traditional tenet of warfare: *"Know Your Enemy."* When fear hits, most people retreat, run, hide, deny, or even cry. These reactions are part of our human nature. However, such reactions only allow the fear to grow and dominate. Fear becomes an *"unjustified terror which paralyzes needed efforts to convert retreat into advance."*

So, how do we break free from fear's paralyzing effects? How do we convert "retreat" into "advance"? First, by identifying the enemy. We must determine what we are afraid of and whether or not we have any reason to be afraid. That is the purpose of *Change is Good* Tool #1 – Ask yourself "What am I afraid of?" and "Why am I afraid?" By answering these questions you will be able to determine *why* you feel as you do and whether or not you have any real cause to feel that way. Using this tool enables you to "know your enemy," the essential first step in dealing with fear and change resistance. For this reason, use this tool whenever you realize you're feeling some form of fear, such as worry, hesitation, anxiety, or concern.

Using Tool #1
Like all of our tools, the proper execution of this first one essentially requires five steps.

Step 1: Write the tool and the questions on an index card.

> ### *"Change is Good" Tool Number One*
>
> *What am I afraid of?*
> *and*
> *Why and I afraid?*

Step 2: Review the tool every day for 14 days by saying it out loud to yourself 20 to 25 times a day.   This helps you focus and be more aware of the feelings of fear that you may experience throughout the day. It also gets you accustomed to saying the tool out loud, which is an important element of the next step.

Step 3: Put the tool into practice any and every time you have reason to do so. In this case, that means whenever you detect that you are distracted, or you feel a wave of negative thought or emotion engulfing you, you should respond by posing these two questions to yourself out loud–*"What am I afraid of?"* and *"Why am I afraid?"* Remember that it is essential for you to say these questions *out loud* so that you can *hear* them, which will help you exert *self-control* over the controlling emotion or fear. Repeating the tool aloud enables you to tap into the power of things heard, the power of the spoken word, to gain and exercise self control. Just hearing your own voice ask the questions *"What am I afraid of? and "Why are I afraid?"* challenges the fear and challenging the fear is the first step toward conquering the fear or resistance. This audible approach helps dispel the rush of emotion accompanying fear, at least long enough for you to gain some sense of self control and logic.

Step 4: Keep a log, in an appropriate notebook, of every instance in which you exercise the tool. You should start a new page for each instance, and on that page note three things – the date and time of day that you felt the fear or negative emotion, what that fear was, and who or what caused or "triggered" the fear.

For example, let's imagine that John, the CEO from an earlier chapter who suspected that Ron was plotting against him, already knew about the fearless leadership tools. If he had, he'd probably have made an entry in his log similar to the one below.

"*Change is Good*" *Tool Number One*
What am I afraid of? and Why am I afraid?
January 12 / 2:30 PM : Began to get nervous because it seemed to me that Ron was acting suspiciously when I came around the corner and found him talking to Fred.

Step 5: At the end of each week, review all the entries in your log. Answer the following questions, *in writing*, for each entry in your notebook, as in the sample below.

- How did I respond or react to this situation?
- What did I experience (think and/or feel) by using this tool in this situation?
- What did I realize (about life, myself, or others) from using this tool in this situation?
- What did I learn (about myself, my business, other people, etc.) from this experience?

"*Change is Good*" *Tool Number One*:
What am I afraid of? and Why am I afraid?

January 12 / 2:30 PM : Began to get nervous because it seemed to me that Ron was acting suspiciously when I came around the corner and found him talking to Fred.
I responded to this by asking myself–out loud–the two questions, to identify the fear and challenge the negative thoughts and feelings.
I experienced relief within five minutes of reciting the tool repeatedly.
I realized that I need to try to befriend Ron to see if my fear is legitimate or unfounded.

> *I learned that I can control what I think and feel when I proac-tively and assertively address the negative thoughts and feelings.*

Applying What You've Learned

Using this tool and conducting a weekly review is beneficial in several ways, both immediately and in the future. The most obvious immediate benefit is that it enables you to determine whether or not your fear or thinking is unfounded.

If your review suggests that your fear is instinctive (versus un-founded fear), that is, that you have good reason to be concerned or cautious, then you will have the advantage of "knowing your enemy" (the fear). And once you have identified what is influencing or even controlling your thinking, behavior, or performance, you'll be able to create a plan of action designed to deal specifically with whatever the danger may be. In such an event, it is advantageous to put the plan *in writing*.

For example, if, in the course of his review, John discovered that Ron really was trying to undermine him, he might devise a plan that read in part:

1. Focus on improving my personal job performance and grow-ing our business— by 15%, *or* by X amount of dollars, *or* with two new customers during the next 90 to 120 days.
2. Identify those individuals who are crucial to my position and my success, and begin a concerted effort to build consensus with them.
3. Include many of these same individuals in my "circle" of in-fluence (i.e., charitable endeavors, social events, job and busi-ness opportunities) in order to get to know them more person-ally and intimately, and to allow them to get to know me.

Although devising such a plan may not guarantee that you'll be able to effectively deal with whatever threat you're facing, *not* doing so will virtually guarantee that you won't be able to affect the changes of attitude and action that needs to be made.

On the other hand, if as a result of the review you realize that your fear is unfounded, you will have taken another step in the quest toward self control, a step that will provide you with two very important bene-fits in the future. First, the fact that the process worked, that as a result of doing it you were able to dispel your fear/resistance, will validate the new behavior you're trying to establish. Consequently, you will be even more energized and empowered to approach whatever fears or negative thoughts you have in the future with determination and tenacity. Second, it will enable you to affirm your own sensibilities. Fear often causes us to question our abilities, thoughts, and decisions. Dispelling those fears reinforces your sense of self confidence and enables you to feel positive and assured about yourself and your de-cision-making/execution abilities again. And as your self confidence increases, your bouts with unfounded fears decreases, and you find yourself reacting in an entirely different way to life, to work, and to those around you!

Identifying why you feel as you do and asking whether or not you have any real cause to feel that way is the first step in dealing with fear. In the next chapter, we continue the process by learning how to be proactive versus reactive.

Chapter 14

Been Down So Long, It Looks Like UP To Me!

Tool/Strategy #2: Be Proactive, Not Reactive

All too often, our decision-making abilities are paralyzed or redirected by unfounded fear, worry or doubt. Proactively making decisions and accomplishing those decisions reduces the power and impact of fear on your thinking and choices. The more *proactive* you are, the less *reactive* and/or passive you will be. The opposite is true as well. The less proactive you are, the more reactive and/or passive you will be.

Those who distance themselves from the influence of fear do so, at least in part, because they develop a habit pattern of accomplishment and achievement. Daydreamers do not fit within this group, but strategic thinkers and people of action do. The proactive group is always thinking, strategizing, planning and figuring out the next few steps. Their motto might be, "No daydreaming," unless the daydreaming leads to a specific, positive idea, result or solution.

Norman Brinker's Proactive Lifestyle

Norman Brinker, the Father of Casual Dining and restaurateur responsible for the growth and success of many well-known restaurants like Chili's and Steak & Ale, is a wonderful example of someone who exhibits a proactive lifestyle. Norman's lifestyle stemmed from a proactive habit that was largely developed in childhood.

Growing up in a rural setting, he loved horses (Norman was known for his equestrian accomplishments). There were instances when Norman would see his neighborhood friends riding their horses. Norman would stand at his fence watching the boys as they rode by. Gripped with the pain of not having a horse for himself to ride with his friends, little five-year old Norman would run behind his father's barn and cry. However, rather than continue to sit by and passively watch his friends, Norman, encouraged by his father, started doing odd jobs for neighbors in order to earn money to buy a horse that he knew was for sale. His father's belief was that if you want something badly enough, you should go out and earn the money to buy it, even at an early age.

After months of hard work and ultimately some skilled negotiating to get the prize's owner to come down on his price, Norman bought his first horse.

Norman pursued several more business ventures during his childhood. Throughout these experiences, Norman developed a habit of proactiveness. He learned to take action and be proactive in response to a desire or need for change. This habit helped Norman become an effective, proactive leader.

Change is Good Tool #2 is designed to help you counteract the influences of fear, worry, and doubt by developing a habit of proactiveness in your life. It consists of the simple phrase, *"Be proactive, not reactive."* By repeatedly exercising this tool, you will overcome the influences of unfounded fear and learn to make decisions, carry them out, resist passivity and procrastination, and become a "do-er" rather than a "daydreamer."

Using Tool #2
Step 1: Write the tool down on an index card.

"Change is Good" Tool Number Two

Be proactive , not reactive

Step 2: Review the tool every day for 14 days by saying it out loud to yourself 20 to 25 times a day. This helps you focus on the idea of being proactive instead of reactive, and helps you become accustomed to thinking proactively and decisively.

Step 3: Put this tool into practice whenever you sense that you are procrastinating, daydreaming, passively reacting to a situation, or avoiding making a decision. As soon as you realize that you are being reactive (or not being proactive), respond by saying out loud, *"Be proactive, not reactive."* Be sure to say this out loud so that you can hear the phrase and maximize the power of the spoken word.

Then make a proactive decision related to this situation. Strive to make one proactive decision each day. Record the decision you made, or write down the possible proactive steps you need to take in order to get a particular task completed. Then get started.

Step 4: Record the date and time of day when you felt the need to use this tool, what you were feeling (overwhelmed, paralyzed, worried, etc.), and who or what caused or "triggered" the feeling. Each time you need to exercise the tool, record the instance in your log notebook, on a new page.

Let's look at an example. Let's say you are always late – late to work, late to appointments, late with paying your bills. Often, the reason that you are late is because you are afraid of failing, which causes you to avoid even getting started on certain projects. You also spend too much time worrying and fretting over the details involved in the preparations, which contributes to your not getting things done on time. You have decided to apply *Change is Good* Tool #2 to your situation, to help you develop proactive habits that will replace your old habits. At some point during the day, you might add the following entry into your log.

"Change is Good" Tool Number Two

Be proactive , not reactive
January 17 / 10:00 AM : Felt overwhelmed and panicky when I remembered a meeting that I have scheduled for next week that I am not yet ready for.

After reciting *"Be proactive, not reactive"* out loud several times, you make the proactive decision to prepare for the meeting right now. You think through and record the steps you have to take in order to have everything ready for your meeting. Then you take that first step.

Step 5: At the end of each week, review all the entries in your log. During your review, record answers to the following questions for

each entry, in your notebook, as in the sample below.
- How did I respond or react to this situation?
- What did I experience (think and/or feel) by using this tool in this situation?
- What did I realize (about life, myself, or others) from using this tool in this situation?
- What did I learn (about myself, my business, other people, etc.) from this experience?

"Change is Good" Tool Number Two

Be proactive , not reactive
January 17 / 10:00 AM : Felt overwhelmed and panicky when I remembered a meeting that I have scheduled for next week that I am not yet ready for.
I responded by saying out loud, be proactive, not reactive, and by writing down the steps I need to take to prepare for the meeting.
I became calmer and experienced a sense of greater control over the situation.
I realized that a panicky feeling can simply indicate that I need to get prepared.
I learned that I can take charge of an unknown situation (the future meeting) and lessen the out=of=control feeling by simply starting and then acting on a plan of action.

Applying What You've Learned

By reviewing the times and situations where you used *Change is Good* Tool #2, you avoid many fears in the first place (such as the fear of failing, or the fear of hurting or offending a friend, or the fear of a bill collector's call). You also build self-respect and self-confidence. Plus, you create a positive self-discipline, and you develop the energy to conquer future fears.

Begin today. Develop a habit of action, accomplishment and achievement. Stop daydreaming. Start doing!

If you are struggling with procrastination due to excessive worry and fear, or are unable to take some risks in your life, the next tool will help. *Change is Good* Tool #3 asks the question "What is the worst that could happen?"

Chapter 15

From Worst to First!

Tool/Strategy #3: What is the Worst That Could Happen?

Change is Good Tool #3 involves asking yourself the question, *"What is the worst that could happen?"* Using this tool helps you evaluate all potential consequences of a particular situation or event that you fear may take place. Most of the time, the consequences are not nearly as bad as the fear and emotion makes you believe. Repeatedly posing this question to yourself reduces the power and impact of the fear at the moment that it is pressuring you, which often dispels the intensity of the fear.

Norman Brinker's Example

Looking further at Norman Brinker, we see how this tool works. Norman's first big opportunity in the restaurant business came with Bob Peterson and Jack-In-The-Box restaurants. In 1957, Bob Peterson owned five of these restaurants and gave Norman the opportunity to manage the enterprise. Ultimately, Norman obtained a 20% stake in the company. During this time Norman married the celebrated tennis champion, Maureen Connelly and had two daughters.

In 1964 Norman's father passed away. This left Norman pondering questions about his own future and purpose. While continuing to work with Jack-In-The-Box, he kept coming back to his desire to own and operate his own restaurant enterprise. With his father's death, Norman asked himself if he would one day reach his elderly years with regrets of never attempting to fulfill his own dream. His answer was yes. There would be regret if he did not at least try.

Thus Norman determined to start his own coffeehouse. He soon went to Bob Peterson and told him openly and honestly of his desire. Peterson tried to get Norman to rethink his decision, especially knowing that Jack-In-The-Box would soon be going public. Norman's stake in the company would be worth millions of dollars after an IPO. However, Norman was resolved to strike out on his own, and sold his shares of Jack-In-The-Box back to the company for $80,000. Though this was not the potential millions he could be getting, it was not a bad return on the initial $3,500 investment he made just six years earlier.

Brink's Coffee House was only modestly successful. Since Norman had tasted real success at Jack-In-The-Box, he would not settle for less. Reluctantly, he sold the coffee shop. While in Phoenix the following year, Norman visited a restaurant called the Cork and Cleaver. He liked its concept so much that he befriended the owners, Peter Green and Tom Fleck. With the desire to own and operate a similar concept in Dallas, Norman openly approached the two owners about a franchise opportunity.

Not interested in franchising but at ease with Norman's openness, the two men invited Norman to visit their restaurant and learn their operations. This he did, and the following year Steak & Ale was born. Steak & Ale became the huge hit Norman wanted.

Regarding this first endeavor into owning his own restaurant, Norman told me one day that *"I always knew that at the worst, if I failed, I could just get a job. So, I really had nothing to lose!"*[3]

Norman was essentially applying *Change is Good* Tool #3. In his case, what was the worst that could happen? Nothing, except that he would have to get a job!

Using Tool #3
Step 1: Write the tool and the question on an index card.

"Change is Good" Tool Number Three

What is the worst that could happen?

Step 2: Review the tool every day for 14 days by saying it out loud to yourself 20 to 25 times a day.

Step 3: Practice using this tool whenever you begin to feel hesitant or fearful about a situation or a major decision or opportunity. Respond to that feeling by saying out loud – *"What is the worst that could happen?"* Pose this question to yourself with a carefree, nonchalant or challenging attitude, and not one of worry or fear. In other words, verbally *challenge* the fear. Then come up with some possible answers to the question.

Step 4: Each time you use the tool during the 14-day period, record the details in your logbook. On a new page, enter the date and time of day you felt the need to use the tool, and write down briefly what you feared and who or what caused or "triggered" the fear, worry or apprehension.

Let's say that at this point in your life, you need to go back to school, either to finish your degree or to get another degree. However, you find yourself paralyzed by the fear of rejection or the fear of failure. You dread having to take the entrance exams. Consequently, you procrastinate or put off the application process, thus dooming your educational pursuits before they begin, and therefore allowing the fear to occur anyway.

So, using this fearless leadership tool, you ask yourself, *"What's the worst that could happen?"* You imagine various scenarios until you are able to envision possible outcomes of applying to college. You decide that the worst thing that could happen is that you do poorly on the entrance essays or exams and don't get accepted, and will have to take some preliminary courses to improve your academic skills before being able to retest and reapply. However, you also realize that even with that worst possible outcome, you still will be closer to achieving your goal and will not be giving in anymore to the fear of rejection. On the other hand, you may actually do well on the exams and essays and get accepted into college and start working toward your degree. You defy the fear, complete the application process and schedule those dreaded entrance exams.

In this scenario, you might add the following entry into your log.

"Change is Good" Tool Number Three

What is the worst that could happen?
January 3 / 2:30 PM : When trying to complete the college application, I feared failing the entrance exams or otherwise being unqualified and therefore rejected by the school.

Step 5: At the end of each week, review all the entries in your log and record answers to the following questions for each entry, in your notebook, as in the sample below.

- How did I respond or react to this situation?
- What did I experience (think and/or feel) by using this tool in this situation?
- What did I realize (about life, myself, or others) from using this tool in this situation?
- What did I learn (about myself, my business, other people, etc.) from this experience?

Fearless Leadership Strategies Tool Number Three
What is the worst that could happen?

January 3 / 2:30 PM : When trying to complete the college application, I feared failing the entrance exams or otherwise being unqualified and therefore rejected by the school.
I responded by asking the question "what's the worst that could happen?" and came up with some possible answers.
I experienced a renewed energy and completed the application process.
I learned that many of my fears have very little basis of truth or fact behind them.

Applying What You've Learned

Using *Change is Good* Tool #3 and reviewing your log throughout the week helps you defy the fear, further build your self-confidence and create a new habit pattern that contradicts fearful, procrastination-prone living. As was true in Norman Brinker's life, what have you got to lose?

The next chapter looks at the fourth tool, and we learn to do the opposite action that the fear is often telling you to do.

Chapter 16

Gut Check

Tool/Strategy #4: Make Yourself Do, Say or Think the Exact Opposite

A key characteristic of fearless, effective leaders and organizations is their ability to stand strong in the face of fear of change and do what is right rather than what the fear is influencing them to do. Faced with failure, friction or fear, they refuse to quit or give up. They literally make themselves do the very opposite of what fear and anxiety normally tells them to do. That is *Change is Good* Tool #4.

A "Change is Good" Organization

Let me tell you about an organization where the rank and file employees are leaders and "Partners," not just employees. Their HR department is referred to as the "People" department and the leadership encourages and pays for employee personal growth through continuing education and leadership development. This organization is consistently ranked by *Fortune Magazine* as one of the 100 Best Places to Work in the nation year after year. With branch offices in several key cities throughout the United States, this unusual organization is headquartered in Dallas, Texas. The company is TDIndustries.

As an organization, TDIndustries exemplifies fearless leadership.

Led by CEO Harold McDowell and President Rod Johannsen, TDIndustries is a leader in the field of commercial, industrial mechanical and electrical construction, service and operations. Their work is found everywhere in structures like Cowboys Stadium, home of the NFL's Dallas Cowboys, The Ball Park in Arlington, home of professional baseball's Texas Rangers, and the American Airlines Center, home of the Dallas Stars professional hockey team and the Dallas Mavericks NBA basketball team.

In addition to their Fortune Magazine annual ranking, TDIndustries has been named National Contractor of The Year by the 18,000 mem-

has been named National Contractor of The Year by the 18,000 member Associated Builders and Contractors. These honors are rightly deserved. TD's leadership believes in team empowerment. They also believe in servant leadership. Its leaders are expected to model servant leadership with all of the company's "Partners," and they do.

TDIndustries believes in people. More specifically, they believe in their people, their "Partners," and it shows. TDIndustries is a progressive company when it comes to investing in its people. According to Jack Lowe, TD's Chairman of the Board, their investment in their people produces tremendous returns.

In Jack's own words: *"Our goal is not to maximize shareholder return. Our goal is to be a great place to work."*

What is the payback for TD? Can this investment in people affect the bottom line? Yes. TD's annual turnover rate for employees with at least three years tenure is *under 1%!*

Conquering Change Resistance

When we speak of conquering change resistance (the fear of change), we are speaking of not letting fear distract or influence sound judgment or decision-making in specific growth and transition situations. Whether it is for individuals or for an entire organization, when it comes to bridling fear's influence, most people will look back and see such instances as defining moments in their life and/or career. When asked about a defining moment in the life of TDIndustries, Jack Lowe describes the events of the company in 1989:

> *"Construction business in the late '80s was difficult. We had expanded in response to those difficulties and had gotten ourselves in trouble in the process. In 1989 we had $10 million in net worth and $5 million in operation losses. Our bank, with whom we owed $15 to $16 million, had failed and was taken over by the Federal Government. Our bonding company, who is critical for us in getting jobs, grew very cautious in treasury bonds. Both of these happened within 90 days. We could not find another bank. We were in serious trouble.*
>
> *There was a lot of anxiety within our leadership. We realistically wondered whether or not we would*

be able to make payroll.

I was scared, but I never confronted the idea of failure. It was trust and determination. It was stressful, but in a lot of ways it was pretty exciting. I just kept going, looking for options, and thinking to myself, 'We can't fail. But how are we going to get through this?'

I did what a triage officer had to do. There wasn't a lot of time for debate.

I talked with friends and peers to get their ideas and input. Then I made a list of things I thought we needed to do. The last item on that list was, 'Don't panic!'

We did everything on that list.

One item on that list was our partners' Defined Benefits Program. It was funded at $5 million at the time. After some research we realized we could cash this policy in and get $1 million with $4 million distributed back to the partners. But we needed another $1 million. So, someone suggested investing some of that $4 million from the partners back to the company. We then worked out a fair-share formula on a sliding scale based on age.

I visited with everyone over the next three to four weeks asking for their support. We raised $1.25 million and saved the company, literally.

However, getting that capital was not the end of it. Our problems did not go away with just that. We also had to sell off some assets.

It was inspiring to watch everyone rally around our cause. We survived and lived to fight another day.

It was at this time that we embraced quality as a standard. This was a defining moment in our turnaround. This situation bound us together. It was like we were saying, 'we are burning the lifeboats!'

We all owned stock valued at $8 to 10 million with

*a payroll of $25 million. So, putting that $1.25 mil-
lion in the context of what was at stake puts the entire
situation into perspective.*

*The reason we got through this together was be-
cause we trusted each other. You can't trust each
other without mutual commitment and integrity."*[4]

Did you notice how Jack Lowe, Jr. responded to fear?   He said,

*"I was scared, but I <u>never</u> confronted the idea of
failure. I just kept going, looking for options and
thinking to myself, 'We can't fail. But how are we going to get through this?'*

*I talked with friends and peers to get their ideas
and input. Then I made a list of things I thought we
needed to do. The last item on that list was, 'Don't
panic!'*

We did everything on that list."

This is a key characteristic of leadership through change in individuals and organizations. Faced with failure, friction or fear, *they
refuse to quit or give up.* They literally make themselves do the very
opposite of what fear and anxiety normally tells a person to do. In es-
sence, they exercise *Change is Good* Tool #4: *"Make yourself do, say,
or think the exact opposite."*

Using Tool #4
   Step 1: Write the tool on an index card.

"Change is Good" Tool Number Four

Make yourself do, say, or think the exact opposite.

   Step 2: Review the tool every day for 14 days by saying it out
loud to yourself 20 to 25 times a day.

   Step 3: Whenever a negative feeling or fear begins to build within you, pause long enough to exercise this tool. Ask yourself, out loud, *"What is this emotion urging me to do, say or think?"* Then, briefly *record* your answer on paper. Next, ask yourself, *"What is the exact opposite thought, action or statement of what this feeling is urging me to do?"* Again, *record* your answer on paper. Then, physically force yourself to carry out or do what you recorded.

As emphasized before, without the writing part of this exercise, it is essentially a waste of time. Habits will not change. Thinking will not change. Performance will not change. So be sure you *record on paper* the answers to these questions.

Here are some examples of "opposite" actions. If the feeling you are experiencing is urging you to clam up, then the opposite action is to open up. If the urge is to verbally blame or attack someone, then the opposite is to assume responsibility and not accuse someone else. If the urge is to think you are going to fail tomorrow, then the opposite is to think that you will succeed tomorrow. If the urge is to *not* make some needed or necessary phone calls, then the opposite is to make those phone calls. Whatever you're feeling, write down first what the feeling is urging you to do, then write down and carry out the opposite of those actions. How do you know that the "opposite" is the right or best choice to make? If the "opposite," *over the long haul*, produces a good end result then it is the choice to go with.

Step 4: Each time you use the tool during the 14-day period, record each occurrence in your logbook. On a new page, enter the date and time of day you felt the need to use the tool, and write down briefly what you were feeling and who or what caused or "triggered" the feeling at that moment.

Let's say that you work at a large company where you do not often have the opportunity to talk one on one with the president or other senior executives. When you do encounter one of these leaders, you tend to avoid conversing with them because of your feelings of inadequacy and/or lack of self-confidence. When you start applying *Change is Good* Tool #4 to your life, you could have an entry in your logbook similar to the following example:

"Change is Good" Tool Number Four
Make yourself do, say, or think the exact opposite.

February 8 / 7:30 AM : I saw the president of the company waiting at the elevator, and my tendency was to slow down so that I would not have to take the same elevator as him.

Step 5: Review all the entries in your log at the end of each week. During your review, record answers to the following questions for each entry, in your notebook, as in the sample below.

- How did I respond or react to this situation?
- What did I experience (think and/or feel) by using this tool in this situation?
- What did I realize (about life, myself, or others) from using this tool in this situation?
- What did I learn (about myself, my business, other people, etc.) from this experience?

"Change is Good" Tool Number Four
Make yourself do, say, or think the exact opposite.

February 8 / 7:30 AM : I saw the president of the company waiting at the elevator, and my tendency was to slow down so that I would not have to take the same elevator as him.
I responded by doing the opposite of what the fears were telling me to do – I purposefully walked up to the elevator and said hello to the president.
I experienced a very interesting conversation with the president throughout the elevator ride and for a few moments in the lobby.
I realized that I can make myself do something I would normally be afraid of doing, with positive results.

Applying What You've Learned

Sometimes you just have to face the flame, bite the bullet, and move forward in spite of the fear and worry about the change or transition. If you've done your homework and research, and the decision makes sense both logically and intuitively, then plow forward. This tool helps to remove your mind away from the clutches of an emotion that leads to limitation, restriction and confinement and toward productive growth and result.

The vast majority of the time, once you've moved beyond the fear, you'll discover that it had no or very little basis of truth behind it, and you will be better off, happier, and more successful with the issue at hand. In the rare instance where moving forward was not the best move (in hindsight), it is still okay and even good, because as a result of moving forward, you grew, matured and learned things you would not and could not have learned if you had remained stuck where you were.

Do you often find yourself asking "what-if..." and thinking the worst about a situation? The next chapter addresses this problem and presents *Change is Good* Tool #5: "Resist What-If Thinking: So what! Who cares? What does it matter? And if it does matter, why does it matter, because it should not matter!"

Chapter 17

Can You Hear Me Now?

Tool/Strategy #5: Resist "What-if" Thinking:
So What, Who Cares, What Does It Matter?

The talented head controller of a fast paced $20 billion technology giant was indispensable to the leadership of his company, and they knew it. However, there was a problem. Despite his best efforts, his supervisor had issues with his performance. There was a lot at stake, not only with his career, but for the company as well. The controller was highly skilled, had a high IQ and knew his tasks well. However, he had difficulties with delegation. On the surface it appeared that he micro-managed; he couldn't let go. Exploration and research into the situation, however, revealed that the real source of the problem was his poor communication skills. And most poor communication problems find their root in fear.

Communication Disconnect

The controller had a preoccupation with what others may say or think about his ideas, and therefore he worried that others may doubt his ability and credibility for the job. Consequently, he did not speak up often enough. His caution caused his peers to question his competency for the job. In other words, the very thing he feared and worried about, he brought upon himself. How? By being so distracted and preoccupied with the fear or worry that he took on behaviors that then caused the people around him to take on the very mindsets that he so readily feared they would have about him in the first place. This is exactly the principle that was discussed in Chapter 5: *"Recognizing Fear"* Is this problem changeable? Sure it is.

By working through specifically assigned tools and exercises, we learned that the head controller needed to build his listening skills (a major facet of communication that many people lack). As we helped him develop several key listening skills, we discovered the root of his communication problems. This controller would *listen* (partially) until he thought he knew where the other person was going or coming from, then he would subconsciously assume what the other party was thinking or intending. He would then base his conclusions and decisions on his own personal, internal *assumptions*, without ever fully listening and then asking for clarification. This is a common communication problem, so I will repeat it:

He would listen until he believed he knew where the other person was going, then he would subconsciously assume what the other party was thinking or intending. He would then base his conclusions and decisions on his own assumptions, without asking for clarification.

This executive was afraid of how others might perceive him. His fear caused him to focus more on what he was *going to say*, rather than on what was *being said*. And at this point in his life, his poor listening methods had become a simple habit.

However, tracing back to the root of the problem, we found that this bad listening habit had its genesis in insecurity and self-doubt, which are rooted in fear. Specifically, fear of:

- being inferior,
- being rejected,
- not being listened to,
- failure,
- inadequate.
- not being valued,
- being wronged,
- of change.

These fears led to self-doubt and insecurity, which led to being pre-occupied with how others perceived him, which caused the controller to become more focused on being heard rather than on hearing and listening to others. Therefore, he did not fully engage his cognitive mind and attention to others when they spoke, he didn't hear nor understand *all* that others communicated, and he acted on his own assumptions.

As simple as this may seem, most people who have poor communication habits will continue with those habits unless they make a concerted, conscious effort to apply training-over-time methods for changing these habits. One tool we used to conquer this bad habit with our controller friend was *Change is Good* Tool #5: *"Resist What-If Thinking: So what! Who cares? What does it matter? And if it does matter, why does it matter, because it should not matter!"* This tool dispels thoughts like:

> *"What if they don't like me,*
> *What if they don't respect me, and*
> *What if they do not listen to me?"*

Once he began to regularly practice this tool, the head controller was a different person. He relaxed. Where once he had been perceived as weak, meek, distant and passive, he now came across as confident, yet interested in others, even proactive, because he was free to be himself. The tool gave him power over the fear's influence.

Using Tool #5
Step 1: Write the name of the tool and the two questions on an index card.

"Change is Good" Tool Number Five

Resist what-if thinking: so what, who cares, what does it matter?

And if it does matter, why does it matter,

because it should not matter?

Step 2: Review the tool every day for 14 days by saying it out loud to yourself 20 to 25 times a day.

Step 3: Whenever you start to doubt yourself or feel inadequate or insecure, exercise this tool. Ask yourself, out loud, *"So what, who cares, what does it matter? And if it does matter, why does it matter, because it should not matter?"* Repeatedly ask yourself these questions until the intensity of the doubt and insecurity diminishes.

Step 4: Each time you use the tool during the 14-day period, record each occurrence in your logbook. On a new page, enter the date and time of day you feel the need to use the tool, and write down briefly what you were feeling and who or what caused or "triggered" the feeling.

For example, if our head controller friend were using this tool, his logbook might contain the following entry:

"Change is Good" Tool Number Five
Resist what-if thinking: so what, who cares, what does it matter, because it should not matter.?

March 8 / 1:30PM: While preparing for the weekly staff meeting, I became worried about my staff's reaction to a new policy that I wanted to implement, and began to seriously doubt the wisdom of the policy.

Step 5: Review all the entries in your log at the end of each week. During your review, record answers to the following questions for each entry, in your notebook, as in the sample below.

- How did I respond or react to this situation?
- What did I experience (think and/or feel) by using this tool in this situation?
- What did I realize (about life, myself, or others) from using this tool in this situation?
- What did I learn (about myself, my business, other people, etc.) from this experience?

"Change is Good" Tool Number Five
Resist what-if thinking: so what, who cares, what does it matter, because it should not matter.?

March 8 / 1:30PM: While preparing for the weekly staff meeting, I became worried about my staff's reaction to a new policy that I wanted to implement, and began to seriously doubt the wisdom of the policy.
I responded by exercising this tool and asking myself the above questions over and over.
I experienced a reduction in my doubt and anxiety, and became confident again about implementing the new policy.
I realized that I second-guess my ideas way too much, and that

---

---

*as the boss, I have the right and the obligation to set policies
that will work best for my team.
I learned that I can counteract doubts and insecurity by exercising this tool and remembering that I am well qualified for what
I do.*

Applying What You've Learned

Because of fear, worry or anxiety, many people doubt and second-guess themselves. Consequently, these people often live on the *defensive*. Whenever someone questions a decision or statement they make, they end up trying to defend themselves. After only a few of these instances, some people will stop making decisions and communicating with others altogether for fear of being challenged. They become preoccupied with self-doubt and insecurity.

When this happens within a group or organization, vital communication, interaction, creativity and actions are suppressed by the very people who have the information that the team needs. In other words, the answers and solutions may already be residing within one or more of the people in the group, team or organization. It is just a matter of getting those answers and solutions to the surface. How do you do that? By teaching the members of the group to apply *Change is Good* Tool #5.

This tool reduces the anxiety of defensiveness, fear of failure, and preoccupation with self. It helps you listen fully to what is being said by others around you. This in turn creates greater confidence and initiative, especially when it is needed most by the team or organization.

Next, we'll discuss the last fearless leadership tool, and learn how to better qualify ourselves to be among the successful.

Chapter 18

Did You Burn Your Draft Card?

Tool/Strategy #6: Many Are Called, But Few Are Chosen: What am I Doing Today to Qualify Myself?

Have you ever felt you were qualified for a better position than the one you currently serve? Have you ever been in a situation where you were better qualified than your boss? Have you ever found yourself better qualified for a promotion than someone else, but they received the promotion instead? If so, this tool is for you.

Change is Good Tool #6 is based on an age-old principle of life: *"Many are called, but few are chosen."* What does this mean? Breaking the principle down into its individual phrases reveals the answer.

Many Are Called

"Many Are Called" means that there are many people who have the ability, skill, talent, and potential to do, be or become something great, powerful, useful. For this reason, they are called: called to service, called to work, called to exercise their ability, called to an opportunity.

Few Are Chosen

"Few Are Chosen", reveals a couple of eye-opening dynamics. First, there is something that happens between the calling and the choosing that dramatically changes things. In other words, *something* occurs that causes a lot of people to *disqualify* themselves by the time they get to the "choosing." That "something" has many terms. Phrases like boot camp, trials, testing, difficulty, wilderness and hardship all come to mind. It is obvious that between the calling and the choosing, some form of challenge or *adversity* occurs within everyone's journey and within every organization's journey that defines the person and/or the organization. Typically these are defining moments.

What determines the defining moment?   Our response to the adversity. How we each *respond* to the trial, testing or adversity either
qualifies or disqualifies us. It is that simple.

Integrity and Character

Many individuals and organizations disqualify themselves simply
because of *how* they respond to their adversities. These challenges are
often disguised opportunities to prove ourselves or to improve ourselves.

However, our human nature entices us to take the easy way out.
Often this easy route includes lying, cheating, deception, cutting corners, or a compromise of character and integrity. On the surface, this
route seems to be the easiest, most painless way to go. But over the
long-haul, it is the absolute worst way to go. In addition, it disqualifies you and your organization from future opportunities.

Determination and Persistence

Another way of disqualification is quitting and giving up. Between the calling and the choosing, many people simply quit or give
up. In over thirty years of experience with working with habits, leadership and human behavior, I can reasonably say that for every one
hundred people who are called, only ten to twenty, at the most, qualify
themselves. In other words, for every one hundred people or organizations that have the potential to do, be and become great and influ-
ential, a full eighty to ninety percent disqualify themselves, either by
compromising their character or by quitting and giving up.

Life is often like boot-camp. It is not always a beach party. Life
requires decisions 24 hours a day (even in your dreams you sometimes
make decisions). How we each choose to respond to life's issues determines whether we qualify or disqualify ourselves. It is never too
late to change your approach to adversity and risk and to qualify yourself to be chosen for the next opportunity.

This last tool helps us counter the influences of fear in our lives:
- the fear of being inadequate or inferior,
- the fear of rejection, and
- the fear of failure or making a mistake.

With this tool, we may *qualify* ourselves for better opportunities.
Change is Good Tool #6 asks the question: *"Many Are Called, But
Few Are Chosen: What am I Doing Today to Qualify Myself?"*

Using Tool #6

Step 1: Write the name of the tool and the question on an index card.

> ### *"Change is Good" Tool Number Six*
>
> *Many are called, but few are chosen.*
> *What am I doing today to qualify myself?*

Step 2: Review the tool every day for 14 days by saying it out loud to yourself 20 to 25 times a day. This will serve to remind you to maintain the right attitude about your situation and not let a personal fear cause you to be a quitter or develop a habit of being a quitter.

Step 3: Exercise this tool each day by asking yourself, out loud, "What am I doing today to qualify myself?" Then, briefly record your answer on paper. Determine to do the right thing, make the right choice, in spite of how it feels. Choose what you know to be the best choice for all concerned over the long haul. Determine to qualify yourself for better, higher opportunities, simply by choosing to act, not react.

A friend, who is currently the CEO of a $200 million food services company, once told me of a time when his career was at an impasse. Some twenty years ago he aspired to a higher position, yet his bosses could not see him fitting in that position. One day he decided he would begin living his life and conducting his business as if he already had the job he aspired to – as if he already had the position. Do you know what happened? Within six months he was promoted to that position! Would it have ever happened if he had disqualified himself with personal fears and feelings of inadequacy or inferiority? Would it have happened if he allowed himself to struggle with fears and feelings of rejection by the superiors who were not promoting him? Would he have been promoted if he had quit in disgust (given up)? Of course not! His promotion occurred because he "qualified" himself by asking himself the question, "What can I do today to qualify myself?" His answer was to begin functioning *as if he already had the job.*

Begin thinking, functioning and acting as if you already are in that promoted position that you aspire to. Start doing for others around you the things you know you'd be doing if only you were where you desire to be. Just start being that person regardless of where you are or how things are at the moment.

Step 4: Each time you use this tool during the 14-day period, record each occurrence in your logbook. On a new page, enter the date and time of day you used the tool, and write down briefly the results of carrying out your plan to qualify yourself that day.

The following illustrates a possible logbook entry for tool #6:

"Change is Good" Tool Number Six
Many are called, but few are chosen.
What am I doing today to qualify myself?

March 2 / 9:30AM: Today I defined what needs to change in order for me to get that promotion.

Step 5: Review all the entries in your log at the end of each week. During your review, record answers to the following questions for each entry, in your notebook, as in the sample below.
- How did I respond or react to this situation?
- What did I experience (think or feel) by using this tool?
- What did I realize (about life, myself, or others)?
- What did I learn (about myself, my business, others, etc.)?

"Change is Good" Tool Number Six
Many are called, but few are chosen.
What am I doing today to qualify myself?

March 2 / 9:30AM: Today I defined what needs to change in order for me to get that promotion.
I responded by writing down what needs to change on paper.
This exercise made me feel good about my ability to affect a positive change in my job and career.
I realized that I don't have to sit back and wait for things to happen. Instead, I can take positive steps to make them happen.
I learned that I am more capable than I tend to think I am.

Applying What You've Learned

Quitting is a choice. It is not inevitable, unless you give it that power. Read through the following events. How would you respond to each of the following events if they happened to you? Would you qualify or disqualify yourself? How would your organization respond?

The following events are *all true* and real. They all happened to just one person. Can you name the individual?

- This person had to work to support his family after the family was forced out of their home.
- His mother died when he was only nine years old.
- He failed at his first effort in business.
- He was defeated in his first attempt at running for legislative politics.
- This person lost his job and could not get into law school.
- He declared bankruptcy and spent the next 17 years of his life paying off the money he borrowed from friends to start his business.
- He was defeated for legislature a second time.
- He was then engaged to be married, but his fiancé died.
- Heart-broken from the loss of his fiancé, he suffered a nervous breakdown and spent the next six months in bed.
- This individual was then defeated in another attempt at politics, this time at running for state legislature.
- He was defeated in becoming elector.
- He then was defeated for US Congress.
- And again defeated for US Congress.
- He was defeated for US Senate.
- This persevering soul was then rejected for the job of US Land Office in his home state.
- He was defeated for US Senate again.
- He was then defeated for Vice-President of the US (received less than 100 votes).
- He was defeated for US Senate a third time.

As we read through this list, I wonder, how many of us would pass on the opportunity to hire (or vote for) this candidate?

- Finally, this individual was elected President of the United States.[5]

Have you figured out the identity of this president? His ascendancy to the highest office in our land came because of several very uncommon and unlikely events. The nation was sharply divided. Our economy was collapsing. The political parties were badly splintered, so much so that the voting public had four choices to choose from for president, not the customary two choices or candidates.

Each of these unique events, all converging at the same point in history, made the unlikely, likely; the election of a politically unproven outsider into the highest office in the land.

Still not sure who this is?

It is important to note that this one man is believed by many to be responsible for the very life and existence of the United States of America today. If for no other reason than this, I believe we can all say that his responses to his adversities conquered the influences of fear in his life and therefore allowed him to *qualify* himself. And because he refused to quit and give up, he was *chosen*.

This chosen man, to whom we all owe a great debt of gratitude, penned these now well-known words during one of the darkest hours of our Nation's history:

> *"Four score and seven years ago, our fathers brought forth upon this continent, a new nation, conceived in liberty, and dedicated to the proposition that all men are created equal.*
>
> *Now we are engaged in a great civil war, testing whether that nation, or any nation so conceived and so dedicated, can long endure. We are met on a great battlefield of that war. We have come to dedicate a portion of that field, as a final resting place for those who here gave their lives that that nation might live. It is altogether fitting and proper that we should do this.*
>
> *But, in a larger sense, we cannot dedicate—we cannot consecrate—we cannot hallow—this ground. The brave men, living and dead, who struggle here, have consecrated it, far above our poor power to*

add or detract. The world will little note, nor long remember what we say here, but it can never forget what they did here.

It is for us, the living, rather, to be dedicated here to the unfinished work which they who fought here have thus far so nobly advanced. It is rather for us to be here dedicated to the great task remaining before us—that from these honored dead we take increased devotion to that cause for which they gave the last full measure of devotion—that we here highly resolve that these dead shall not have died in vain—that this nation, under God, shall have a new birth of freedom— and that government of the people, by the people, for the people, shall not perish from the earth."[6]

You know the rest of the story. These are President Abraham Lincoln's immortal words known as The Gettysburg Address. In the face of immense hardship, suffering and difficulty, President Lincoln did not disqualify himself. His proactive, unwavering response to the very real fear and threat of the breakup of the United States of America qualified him, not only for another day, but for generations to come.

You never know what the full impact of your own choices will be when you determine to qualify yourself through right responses to adversities, worries and concerns especially worry or fear about an upcomng change. *Embrace opportunity amidst uncertainty.* Do not allow fear and more specifically, the fear of change, to limit or hold you or your organization back.

PART FOUR

What follows is a compilation of assorted, yet essential material for the reader who is serious about facilitating authentic change within his or her own situation – whether it be with an individual, group, or organizational basis.

Chapter 19

Change & Fear:
Two Organizations, Two Fates

Change and Change Resistance

Change. The human creature resists change. Although our resistance to change comes from a primal survival instinct, in today's world economy, allowing this primal instinct to completely control us often leads to our own peril or demise as we shield ourselves from the very things that allow us to grow and prosper.

As we have discussed in these pages, we resist change because of the emotion of fear; fear of change, fear of the unknown, etc. However, life and growth, be it organic or inorganic (man-made), requires change. Over the centuries, countless species have come and gone. Those that adapted well to their environment survived to pass those traits to their offspring. Those that failed to change, or were too slow to change, died out. Our bodies survive through a process called Cell Regeneration, or Cell Turnover. Through this process new cells are constantly created to replace old ones. Over a period of about nine years most of the cells in your body are replaced. But as we get older, this process slows down. Over time, as we age, our body stops creating newer cells until we eventually die. In other words, *without change we die*. Death stops change dead in its tracks.

On the other hand, in business, a strategy of growth embraces change because change is a good, healthy sign of growth and life. This strategy assumes change and factor's in the forces of fear and emotion on the human mind and consequently incorporates tools and tactics that will assist the people involved in the change process. Such tools and tactics can come in many forms; incentives, culture, opportunity, etc.

The Pursuit of A Dream

In the 1980s an aspiring young businessman incorporated these variables into his vision and strategy. His initial objective was to start, build and run a successful enterprise. This sounds simple enough.

However, his first idea met with failure. He had a vision for selling time shares in business aviation - fractional ownership for air travel. The market wasn't ready for this young entrepreneur's vision and although the marketplace would be ready for this concept a decade later, his idea failed. This defeat created the emotional burden of failure within the young businessman. For most of us the pain of failure lingers within our consciousness far longer than the pleasure of success, rendering us reluctant to try again – and many never do.

However, by the mid-1980's, this young enterprising soul arose from his loss, brushed the failure residue off of his clothes and began anew with another business idea. This time, his efforts found success as he partnered with another in real estate development. But again, within just a couple of years, through no fault of his own, this enterprising young man faced failure as the National economy turned south. The economic downturn was devastating and ruinous to millions of people and this entrepreneur was not immune. As a matter of fact, the down-turn in the economy proved so damaging to his business that he lost almost everything and was brought to the edge of bankruptcy.

But this is where the story gets better, much better.

Right Time, Right Place, Right Opportunity

Again aligning himself in a partnership, our aspiring businessman set out to give his dream a *third* attempt. This time however, instead of either starting from scratch (the fractional ownership of aircraft idea) or being involved in a business and industry whose pulse was too closely tied to the waves of the business cycle (real estate development), our subject made the fateful decision to buy an existing enterprise, one that already had decades of history and one that already had a proven track record; meaning:

- years of annual profits,
- a solid customer base, and
- an already existing market for its product.

With financial partners, our resilient soul sought an existing business that met his strategic criteria. This was the late 1980s. The Savings and Loan crisis had triggered a national economic downturn that littered the business landscape with dead and dying corpses. One company on the brink of extension was Southland Corporation. You may recognize them by their more public moniker, 7-11 Convenience Stores. Southland was on the brink of bankruptcy at the time.

In an attempt to survive the carnage of the economic tsunami of that day, Southland was selling off valuable but non-core assets in order to raise cash. One of those assets happened to be the very business that was responsible for 7-11's beginnings back in the 1930s; Ready-Ice. Ready-Ice was a packaged ice business that had proven so successful over prior decades that it spawned many competitors. However, on this day, Ready-Ice was about to be orphaned, jettisoned from Southland's stable as the parent company's singular focus was on the survival of their core business, the convenience store operations.

Enter our aspiring entrepreneur with two failures on his resume. Backed by a partnership that brought both financial and intellectual capital to the table, Gregg Engles bought Ready-Ice for $26 million. Most of the purchase price was borrowed and it's been said that the initial $100,000 down payment was also in borrowed funds. Today, Gregg presides as the CEO over Dean Foods, an $11 billion dollar dairy company ranked #208 on the Fortune 500 list (2011). How did Gregg grow $26 **million** dollar Ready-Ice into $11 **billion** dollar Dean Foods in just 13 years?

It began with an idea married to a strategy that required constant, consistent, continuous *change*.

Embracing Change, Change is Good

The idea was to acquire a solid business that had growth potential. The strategy was to grow that business through M&A's, all the while factoring in the balancing act between the motivation and performance of the human capital and the fear and change resistance within the tens of thousands of employees amidst a rapidly growing company.

With Ready-Ice firmly within his reins, over the next five years Engles acquired and merge into Ready-Ice over a *dozen* additional ice-manufacturing and distribution companies. Through the consolidation of facilities and the creation of greater economies of scale, Gregg established a solid, secure pattern of accelerated growth. Noticing Engle's formula for success in the early 1990's, one of his mentors suggested Engle's apply the same M&A framework to the dairy industry. At the time, the dairy industry was ripe for the consolidation and melding of operations. For decades most of the nation's larger dairies were family owned and operated. These were people of good stock, high character, and strong work ethic, the type of people with whom Engles readily identified with as he held similar values for himself.

However, these dairy enterprises were also a splintered group throughout the national landscape; a fragmented industry filled with wasteful redundancy and duplication. Having witnessed the potential reward for lean operations and economies of scale through his Ready-Ice growth strategy, Engles overlaid a similar plan onto his venture into the dairy industry.

And so the next phase of this successful enterprise commenced in 1993 with the $99.4 million dollar acquisition of Suiza Dairy Corporation of Puerto Rico.

What was Engles' secret formula for success? It really is not that much of a secret. As a matter of fact, the strategy has been around for some time and such juggernauts as Warren Buffet, J.P Morgan, Andrew Carnegie, and Cornelius Vanderbilt have employed the same if not similar strategy over the past two centuries.

All of these men of fortune followed a similar pattern:

> ➢ Seek out leading companies or business opportunities within a specified region or industry of interest,
> ➢ Make sure they are staffed by strong management teams that can be left in place to insure:
>   • a seamless transition,
>   • the retention of expertise and experience, and
>   • the continuity of continued business relationships.
> ➢ Find and secure additional acquisitions in the same region or industry of interest,
> ➢ Increase market share, efficiencies, and profits through those strategic acquisitions,
> ➢ Continue the growth through innovation and refinement of the core business,
> ➢ Successfully manage change resistance within self and others at every turn, and
> ➢ The ability to simultaneously manage all of these variables on an on-going basis.

And therein lays the issue; because the ability to successfully execute on the management of such variables is a rarity. Many have tried and failed at this model. Few have done it successfully.

The result of successfully executing this tried and true formula was that Engles grew Suiza Foods from a $100 million enterprise in 1993 into the $11 **billion** dollar Dean Foods dairy conglomerate that it is today. He accomplished this through the artful and strategic integration of no less than 45 acquisitions; along the way acquiring such brands as Borden, PET, Meadow Gold, Oak Farms, Land-O-Lakes, Foremost, T.G. Lee, Garelick, Dean's, International Delight, Horizon Organic, and Silk. Today, Dean Foods is the Nation's largest dairy foods company.

Throughout this growth spurt, it can be said that Engles successfully pulled off this feat through the continuous navigation of change management as it pertains to the human capital landscape and their every-changing environment within the enterprise.

As an outsider looking in, I was fortunate enough to witness the merger of Suiza Foods with Dean Foods in 2001. I was there on the twelfth floor (one of two executive suites at that time) developing senior executives. The electricity in the air at the Suiza Foods headquarters was palpable and inoculating. It was an exciting place to be for sure as everyone was not only open to change, but embracing change and all of the anticipated opportunity it was about to bring.

Resisting and Avoiding Change

On the other side of the business landscape world, it just so happened that while I was spending portions of my weeks within the bowels of the executive think-tank at Suiza/Dean Foods in 2001, I was concurrently spending a portion of my time within the halls of the Big Five accounting firm, Arthur Andersen and its Dallas offices. In 2001, Arthur Andersen was an organization of 85,000 employees worldwide with $9 billion dollars in annual revenue. Arthur Andersen's reach affected the majority of the Fortune 1000 landscape and therefore affected millions of lives and billions of GDP.

As Enron's accounting firm caught in the wake of the Enron scandal at the dawn of this century, Andersen was square in the crosshairs of a Federal investigation. In the end, one group of people, Andersen's Houston office, inevitably determined the final fate of a worldwide 85,000 employee organization. It was rumored that the Andersen partners in the Houston office had a track record of arrogance and being above the law. If this was the case, then they made decisions *long before* that fateful year that determined their fate and the fate, future and finances of tens of thousands of others when it came time to "answer for their deeds" during that Federal investigation.

In an attempt to preserve their way of conduct (change resistance), they shredded documents in an attempt to cover-up their accounting practices. Once this act was discovered by the authorities, criminal prosecutorial actions were initiated and within an amazingly short six month period of time, the firm that stood for almost 100 years was brought down and dismantled. One of the largest, most prosperous, most prestigious business organizations in the world was forever removed from the business landscape.

Fear was everywhere within the Dallas offices of Arthur Andersen in 2001. What I witnessed was people who'd spent decades building careers, investing their intellectual capital in their organization, found themselves out of work with a significant portion of their identity forever serving as a footnote in business history. A few individuals in a Houston office made some very bad decisions that brought down an entire worldwide organization.

In the end, those few in that Houston office *resisted* a change of attitude and integrity. And in their attempt to cover up and therefore preserve their way of life and that attitude, a way of life characterized by greed and arrogance, their self-preserving decisions destroyed the livelihoods of many others. Don't let this be your fate. Don't let your resistance to change hinder your opportunities, even when the result may not be what you want.

The Benefits of Change

Conversely, do you think Gregg Engles enjoyed failing at his first two ventures in business and facing the consequences of those failed decisions? Of course not. But he was willing to change whatever he needed to change in order to realize his vision of owning and operating a successful enterprise.

Think about the emotional as well as the financial toll this must have had on this young, aspiring businessman at that point in his career; two failures and no wins right out of college and law school, not a very promising track record so far. Like all of us, Gregg could have resisted change and allowed his feelings and fear of more failure to control his next move. However, he did not respond to the painful result of his first couple of business decisions/actions in this way. He faced the feelings and fears head-on, made adjustments; in short, *he changed.* And then he proceeded to build one of the most dynamic, profitable and needed enterprises in our national business landscape today.

Be open to the dynamics of change. Constructive, strategic change leads to growth and opportunity. Resist fear, embrace change, and enjoy the ride!

Chapter 20

TLS ADAM Change Map™

TLS-T3 Training-over-Time Globe™

First, two of our core tools are the TLS-T3 Training-over-Time Globe™ model and the TLS ADAM Change Map™. These two tools have served as frameworks for much of our change management and leadership development training and work over the past decade. It is primarily because of these two framework tools that we have experienced the results accomplished.

The TLS-T3 T-o-T Globe™ provides the framework for the first stage of any and all individual, group, and organization-wide change. Within the TLS-T3 T-o-T Globe™ framework are the three core essentials for achieving substantive results:

- Training,
- Tools, and
- Time.

Like the spokes of a wheel, when any one of these three components is missing from a change process or development program the end result of the entire project is at risk. Conversely, when a Change Initiative contains structured training that is coupled with substantive behavioral modification tools, and these two then are combined with the element of time, then the opportunity to facilitate and realize genuine, authentic change is greatly enhanced. The TLS-T3 T-o-T Globe™ framework is an efficient yet powerfully effective tool for smaller-scale situations such as individual Leadership Development or Departmental Transformation.

TLS ADAM Change Map™

Similarly, when the TLS ADAM Change Map™ is overlaid onto the TLS-T3 Globe™ we have an efficient yet powerfully effective change agent tool for large-scale projects and circumstances such as full scale M&A integration or full scale Turnarounds. In addition to

the framework components provided by the T-3 T-o-T Globe™, the
ADAM Change Map™ adds seven key steps to the change process
framework:

- Acclimate,
- Analyze,
- Design,
- Deliver,
- Audit,
- Adjust, and
- Master.

TLS ADAM Change Map™

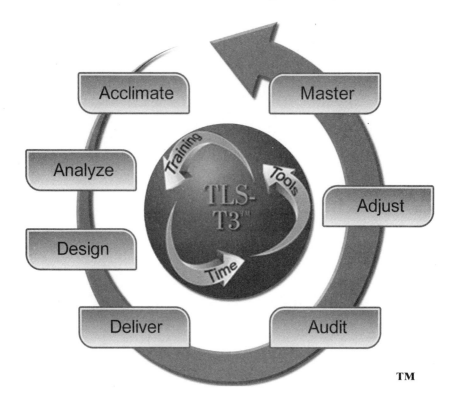

TM

Project Deployment: The TLS ADAM Change Map™

Phase I - "Acclimate"
   Preliminary Agreements

Phase II - "Analyze" & "Design"
   Needs Analysis, Leadership Audit, and Interviews

Phase III - "Deliver" & "Audit" & "Adjust"
   Implementation and Tool Deployment

Phase IV - "Master"
   Follow-up and Maintenance

Chapter 21

When Change Is Necessary

Affecting Change at the Leadership Level

Affecting Change Through Your Leadership Style And Presence

People resist change. They cling to the familiar. It is a centuries old dilemma wrapped around our genetic human survival code. However, as we well know, change is inevitable, especially in a growth environment. Growth encompasses change. Achievement of any kind requires change. So, if you are healthy, change is good.

How do you get an organization, a team, or an individual to embrace and support change?

Brad is the managing general partner of a mid-sized professional services firm. He was recruited into the firm out of college and progressed up the firm throughout his career. With the senior partners retiring, now being a senior partner himself, Brad one day finds himself as the head of the firm. Brad is a very likeable person. It is a strength of his that helped him build a large relationship-oriented clientele over a two-decade period of employment. However, how does Brad's "strength" now translate into his very visible leadership role? Will some take him as soft and seek to manipulate or take advantage of his kindness and empathetic manner? In those times when some tough decisions must be made about an underperforming individual or an underperforming arm of the organization, how does Brad respond?

The answer is two-fold.

First, to affect subtle change within the entire organization, Brad must adjust, alter, or change some small aspect of his leadership style or presence.

It doesn't take much for you to shift or change one small item about your own leadership style or presence. Doing so translates into potentially significant benefits for individuals and for the organization as a whole. Small changes; an action, an initiative, a comment, can have

significant impact on those under your charge because as a leader, you
are being both watched and followed. Your example means a lot.

In your position, you know there are some attitudes and behaviors you'd like to see changed or reversed within some of the people
around you.

So, here is how the one in leadership can affect that change:

a. **On paper**; record *your* perception of your leadership style and
   presence there at your office,

b. **On paper**; now record what you believe is *others'* opinion or
   view of you and your leadership style, -- if you have past tangible feedback of others' perception of you, use that for this
   "b" portion of the tool.
   Both of these should be a list of specific attributes, qualities
   and characteristics that sum up you and your leadership.

c. **Now** make **a third list** of 2, 3 to 5 (no more than 5) behaviors
   you'd most like to see exhibited within the culture *and* people
   of your business that are not currently being exhibited to the
   degree that you wish them to be.

d. **Now**, using only one sheet of paper, put the "a" and "b" lists on
   the far left side of the page and put the "c" list on the far right
   side of the page. In the middle there should be space for a 4th
   column, a blank space for now.

e. **Now**, reviewing both left and right side columns, answer this
   question (placing your answers in the middle or 4th column):

What one thing from the left columns can I slightly, subtly adjust or
change that will lead to one of the items listed on the far right column?

Repeat this question 3-4 times coming up with 3-4 subtle things
you can change or adjust within your own style that will affect and
even impact others in the organization to change their behavior and
ultimately their performance.

Affecting Change Within An Individual

Brad also needs to address an underperforming individual at the
partner level. Law firms, accounting firms, and consulting firms are in
the people business. Their business is to serve their clientele. Therefore it is a necessity that they have clientele to serve. One typically
moves up to the partner level because of the client relationships he or
she has developed throughout his or her career. So, what do you do
with an underperforming partner. Terminating the relationship is the

easy answer. However, being who he is, that is not Brad's first choice. He wants to expend all possible options to see if there is a way to turn this underperforming partner, not necessarily into a star, but at least into a solid, client-centered performer.

With our underperformer in question, Brad, has an opportunity to do and create something really special here for both the firm and for the underperformer and his family. The reason I know this is because what the underperformer had to conquer 8 years prior (through our initial coaching encounter with him) was far more difficult for a trainee to accomplish than what is needed now (being more proactive with developing new business and interacting with people from a business development perspective).

So, here is how the one in leadership can affect that change within another individual:

a. **Make a list** of the specific behaviors you wish to see improved, or changed or eliminated within the trainee. In this instance, being better at developing new client business.

b. Once you have a "workable" list, **select just one item** on that list. It is easy to mess this up if you are too involved, too emotional in the situation. But if you are focusing on the right items that require change, it is rather simple, as long as you are patient.

c. Now with that one item, it becomes a short-term, **mini-goal or objective**.

d. Give the trainee **an assignment** that requires him to carry out that item. If you can make the assignment fun, enjoyable or gratifying that will make this process go much better and much easier.

e. The trainee is to then **report back to you** his or her progress and results **7 days** later.

f. The trainee must record his results and experiences **ON PAPER** and bring two copies to discuss; one for you and one for him or her.

⇨ This will be their **Action Log**. With this action log, be sure they understand that they are to record three things PER ATTEMPT:

    **the date and time of day,

    **who he/she was interacting with and what were the circumstances, and

    **what did he/she learn or realize from this attempt?

g.   Require at least **ONE attempt per day** in-between your weekly "coaching" meetings.

h.   Then, after the trainee has successfully performed this task, move to the second item on your list and repeat the above process, then the 3rd and 4th and so-on.

If Brad does this correctly and remains consistent in every way; weekly meetings, day and time, objectives for doing this exercise, etc. then he will see his underperformer experiencing transformative behavior before your very eyes and that is a VERY good thing to witness.

As long as the trainee is motivated to do the work, the motivation does not have to be because they want to improve…it can be as a result of a negative motivation, "I don't want to lose my job"…, as long as the trainee is motivated and they are supplied with the right tools and given an increased sense of greater accountability for executing on the tools and assignments, then you typically will see that individual change the indentified behaviors over a 2 to 12 month period of time.

Chapter 22

Training-over-Time;

How and Why It Works

TM

To succeed at a change or integration process as an individual, team or organization, you have to address and incorporate the basic drives and needs within the human creature.

The Problem
Improved human performance through change is the byproduct of authentic training and development. Most of what passes for training (seminars, lectures, and many forms of coaching, etc.) is *not* training at all. When a transition through change matters, authentic training

begins with the end in mind. In other words, authentic training has a
clear-cur, clearly defined vision, direction and path, *and* it supplies
the tools to get to that end objective. Most training is insufficient because it falls short of delivering the end result needed and this often is because of the absence of a clearly defined vision and path.

What is the difference between most forms of corporate teaching/
training and Training-over-Time training? The former tells you *what*
the situation is or may be. It may also tell you *why* the situation exists.
The latter *shows* the individual and/or team "*how*" to change and/or
improve their situation.

Teaching's Shortcomings

Another way of looking at it is that teaching tells you *what* you need,
that you need a road map and that you are at point "A." Teaching also
tells you *why* you need a road map, to get to point "B. However, most
forms of corporate teaching/training do not:

1. give you the equipment, *the tools,* to make the trip or journey
   of change, nor do they
2. *experientially* walk you through the initial experiences of that
   change process (getting from point "A" to point "B").

Coaching's Shortcomings

Many forms of coaching offer the opportunity to experientially walk
you through situations, however, coaching is often void of either:

1. The roadmap needed for the change process, or
2. *How* to make the needed changes (the specific steps needed
   for getting from point "A" to point" B").

The Solution

What is the answer? What determines authentic training that produces long-term results? Two dynamics regularly accompany authentic training; a Training-over-Time training model, and definable, time-
tested Tools that produce or facilitate the changes needed.

Training-over-Time

To genuinely address a change in human performance or thinking
we have to strike at the core of what drives human performance and

behavior; **habits**. The human creature is a creature of habit. We have habits in four basic areas;

1. mental thought patterns,
2. emotions, feelings and fears,
3. verbal habit patterns, and
4. physical habit patterns.

Studies tell us that the vast majority of our habit patterns are developed during the first five years of our lives. In other words the experiences we encounter over a five year period develop into habits. Those habits then develop our thinking and behavior. Now, if it takes five years during the most fertile time of our lives to create and develop a habit, why then do we think we can change that habit in just a few hours (through a seminar lecture or a few coaching sessions), or over a weekend (through a retreat or seminar)?

Common sense reveals the futility of this notion. However, individuals and organizations continue to allocate and spend over $50 billion on an annualized basis on processes that have time and again proven themselves to be at best, less than effective.

Our habit development during toddlerhood encompassed two dynamics:

1. Training-over-Time (five years of repetition), and
2. Tools, solutions or ideas practiced or thought about repetitively over time.

These two in tandem, formulate, produce and develop our habit system. Our habit system then determines our behavior. Our behavior produces or determines our interpersonal capability and this capability determines our approach and outlook on people, work and life, which then determines our performance. Our performance determines our degree of success and accomplishment through life's journey.

If we are going to invest in our people, let's use common sense. Invest the organization's resources in training that produces genuine, long-term change. Invest in training that genuinely increases the value of your human capitol. Invest in Training-over-Time training that supplies time-tested Tools for genuine, long-term habit change. Invest with the desired end result in mind.

Chapter 23

When Things Go Wrong;

How Fear and Bias
Effect Decisions

When it comes to assessing blame for a fatal failure within an organization, senior management's circumstance is a lot like that of an aviation pilot's; highly skilled, good at what they do and the first to be blamed when the ship goes down. However, assessing cause to the result is often subtle and hidden. In the end, yes, the success or failure ultimately rests on senior management's shoulders. However, to turn the ship around, one must be willing to look beyond the surface and peer beyond the obvious. In aviation, rarely is it an isolated event or decision that creates a fatal mistake. So it is in the business of managing and navigating a successful enterprise. Usually it is a series of seemingly small, insignificant factors and decisions that, combined, lead to failure.

To ultimately find the true cause of the miscue, it is essential to explore *where* and *how* a firm allocates its resources (time, people and capital). Where, how, to whom, and on what are your organization's resources expended? These key decisions often determine the fate of the organization because these fundamental decisions typically determine:

- ➤ innovation,
- ➤ products to be delivered, and
- ➤ services delivered to customers.

Good pilots typically must manage multiple tasks simultaneously; fuel, airspeed, altitude, power-plant , etc. In this same way, good managers are also typically attuned to the pulse of their customers, constantly monitoring their needs. Therefore a good manager's decisions are often primarily influenced *by* their customers. Subsequently, good managers have a tendency to:

- Listen to their customers,
- Monitor their competitors' actions,
- Invest necessary resources toward higher-performance that will better serve their customers, and
- Produce higher quality products or services in order to achieve a greater profit.

In addition, good managers also attempt to guide their people to focus their energies on activities that:

a. address customers' needs,
b. promise higher profit margins,
c. are realistic to deliver, and
d. help grow the organization's market share.

However, is it this simple? We wish it were. There is more complexity to the resource allocation decision-making process than this, isn't there.

Who and/or what really controls the process that determines what a firm delivers?

There are three core factors that control where, when, how, to whom, and for what an organization allocate its time, people and capital. These three core factors are:

1. Your customers,
2. Your middle managers, and
3. Your personal fears.

Are you fully aware of the intricate variables laden within each of these three core factors? Additionally, are you aware of how these three variables influence your firm's decision-making process; the allocation of your firm's time, people and capital?

1.   Your customers

You are in business to meet customer needs. You invest in what your customer wants. A successful enterprise depends on:

> ➢ Knowing their customers' current and future needs,
> ➢ Identifying the products and/or services that best meet those needs, and
> ➢ Investing resources (time, funds, intellectual capital, etc.) to develop and provide those products and services.

Consequently, *your customers* often determine (knowingly or unknowingly) where, when, how and to what extent your firm chooses to allocate its time, people and capital.

2.   Your middle managers

Many executives are often unaware of the extent to which their middle managers influence this decision-making process.

Although, it is often senior management who decides whether or not to fund a project, this is only after many others at lower levels within the organization have already decided which project proposals *they* will present to senior management for approval. Consequently, senior management typically only sees a subset of the ideas generated by middle management.

How do middle-managers and non-executives make their project proposal decisions?

Often, middle-managers decide which projects they will propose to upper-management based on:

   a.   *Their own* comprehension of what types of projects are most profitable to their employer, and

   b.   *Their belief* in the likelihood of being able to successfully sell the project proposal to upper-management.

Next, (and this is a crucial piece) combined with this is a ***middle-manager's** belief* of how their sponsorship of specific proposals will *affect* their own career trajectories. Individuals' career trajectories accelerate when they sponsor highly successful projects and programs. Of course this is self-serving. However, it is human nature. Consequently, it is and always will be a key component in the decision-making process for resource allocation.

The end result of this process within middle managers is that biases *below senior management's control*, then affect senior management's decision-making opportunities. Even with the best of intentions, business opportunities are restricted by biases below the senior executive level. Do you see how this happens? It is a very powerful component in the decision-making process for resource (time, people, and capital) allocation.

3.   Your personal fears

This variable is often heavily influenced by the first; the customer and their needs. The *fear* of cannibalizing sales of existing products and/or services is often a reason why firms delay introductions. Wrong initiative or direction is another reason why companies delay action that can prove profitable. Fear often breeds caution and then a delayed action as one steps back to re-think or more thoroughly reconsider a decision or course of action. When this happens, to ease the fear (or emotion) we often work first to either:

> a.   Build some sort of consensus that supports our thinking or decision. This can be healthy, but only *if* those in the loop can and do provide genuine, authentic, and complete objectivity to the process, which, because of the personal biases describe above, is often difficult to accomplish.

> b.   Or, we wait to see some sign of promise or hope that our idea will succeed. This typically takes the form of a competitor bringing your idea, service or product to market first. When you wait for your competitor to first deliver in order for you to have your confirmation to proceed, it is too late. Your fear has then become a self-fulfilling prophecy and you are late to market. *You have missed your window of opportunity to be first to market.*

In order to survive and thrive for another day, which means making the best decisions *available,* it is imperative that the successful enterprise factors in the nuances within these three core factors; customers, middle management, and your own fears.

When I Have A Granddaughter

(closing excerpt from the Keynote speech "Change is Good" by Kevin Turner)

Change can be a scary thing. So when I have a granddaughter, instead of "grandfather" she's going to call me Pa. Because I called my grandfather Pa. And I always knew that no matter what happened, Pa was ALWAYS there for me.

And there is one thing we know we can ALL depend on and that's CHANGE. And the first time she realizes that whether she likes it or not, change is coming , I'll make sure she knows she doesn't have to weather that storm alone.

Because change can be a scary thing, especially when you have to endure it alone. But no matter how wide the approaching storm appears to be, I will remind her that "this too shall pass." Because like all storms; storms come and storms go. Nothing lasts forever.

And "Sweetheart," I will tell her, "Don't think the approaching storm won't affect you. Because it will. It will change you. But it will change you for the better because storms have a way of cleansing the air of all that makes life reek.

And remember that after the storm you will want to reach out and fill your lungs to capacity with the fresh air that comes after a cleansing rain. Because it is the fresh new air that reminds you that 'all things are possible,' that the hopes and dreams you've held on to for so long can now take root, and grow – to unforeseen heights, and at dizzying speeds, if only you will allow them."

I want her to see the storms in life for what they really are; opportunities for growth and change.

"And Sweetheart," I'll tell her, "Don't you get too comfortable with today because today's comforts lead to complacency. And complacency is always a painful death of the senses – of everything that's important to you. Instead, fix your sites on tomorrow. And with passion and enthusiasm, embrace the changes that always come with tomorrow. For with tomorrow always comes a new opportunity, if only you will get up off of your comfort zone and pursue change!"

By Kevin Turner, author of
Change is Good

APPENDIX

Q&A With TLS President, Kevin Turner

As an executive trainer/coach you develop executive talent. How do you describe your profession?

In the 1930s management consulting was not considered a profession. Marvin Bower took over McKinsey & Co. and set out to make consulting a "profession" much like that of a lawyer, accountant or doctor. Today we see a similar problem with executive training, performance development, and change management. The function is not treated or considered as a profession. Yet, for all that is at risk in the absence of effective change, executive training is and should be considered a profession. However, if executive training is to be a profession this then lends itself to a couple of problematic issues that must be addressed. First, good, seasoned training professionals don't grow on trees. The "profession" of executive training, performance development and change management is in great need of qualified practitioners. With or without formal academic credentials, it is difficult to find qualified training professionals who:

a.   See their job/vocation as a professional career and therefore are committed to their profession long-term, and

b.   Have the skill, discipline, logical thinking ability, and the intuitive sense to produce the results demanded today for executive development and organizational change within a global economy.

This is not to say our country's graduate programs are not attempting to fill the need for executive trainers. However, they tend to produce graduates who are deep in theory and weak in application. The concept of apprenticeship is not new. Some form of apprenticeship is required for medical doctors, for teachers, and even for auto mechanics. However, we are hard-pressed to find similar requirements for the professional in the executive leadership role. Yet, it is business that makes economies function, grow and thrive and for some reason we as societies, see no need to develop professional trainers in the same way that we develop auto mechanics, teachers or medical doctors.

The second problematic issue is with our training vehicles. For decades business has relied on ways and means of training delivery that have been proven time and again to be inefficient and ineffective. I am speaking of motivational speeches, one-day or week-end seminars, and workshops. I am not against these vehicles. However, when they are being used as a surrogate for executive training and performance development then we are misappropriating critical resources and we are setting valued executives up for failure (and then when the executive does not measure up to the needed standard we blame them, not ourselves or the training vehicle we sent them to).

Companies around the world continue to funnel over $50 BILLION dollars annually into these ineffective modes of training when we already know they do not pro-

duce long-term, measurable human performance change and benefit. They may
work short-term. However, consider this… what other investments are made in a
business enterprise that are made solely for short-term results? Not many, unless
it is to save or salvage in the immediate, the long-term viability of the enterprise.
So, why do we as business leaders continue to approve such enormous expenditures on such short-term results with our most important commodity; our people
and their performance?

Adults do not learn the same way they did when they were children. Adults learn
best by incrementally receiving small portions or "bites" of information, insight or
learning over long, designated, periods of time along with the ability to apply those
"bites" of information into their circle of influence, work and life on a daily basis.
As the adult trainee applies the "bite" into her or his life, it is through that practical
application of the "bite' that the "bite" becomes revelational and transformational
and then, human performance *changes* because thinking, behavior and habit have
changed. Adults need time to absorb what they learn, put it into practice, think
about it as they practice it and then internalize new patterns of thinking and behavior; which then needs to be supported, encouraged and rewarded.

In over 30 years of applying our craft in the profession of executive training and
performance development, what we have learned is that if adult learning is to take
place in a long-term and transformative sense, then it:

1. Must be carried out over a series of learning/training "sessions" (versus
    a one hour , one day, or one weekend event), *and*

2. There must be sufficient time in-between sessions for the trainee to prac-
    tice and absorb each training "bite" of information along the way, *and*

3. The training materials must be *well-prepared* as well as *tailored* to the
    specific needs of the individual trainee, *and*

4. Must have a system of human contact and support throughout the train-
    ing engagement. Learning is digested best when supported by other hu-
    mans the trainee interacts with on a regular basis; be it a team, *or* the
    trainee's trainer/coach, and the trainee's work superior and peers; for
    cultural support.

Our experience has taught us that when these "four steps" are in alignment
for an executive trainee, she or he then has the best likelihood of a successful
training – learning engagement result. And it begins with an experienced, talented
professional who is committed to the profession of executive training/coaching,
performance development, and change management.

**You've said your parents' divorce when you were five, made you who you
are today. How so?**
Well, first, I've always loved competition and business. I couldn't wait until I
was of legal age to work (I believe the legal age was 15 back then). So, I started a lawn mowing business when I was 11. Before that, I can remember always
looking for ways to make money as far back as I can remember. I pestered my
father and grandfather to let me help them and their workers in the farm fields

when I was six and seven (years later I regretted that as by your teen years you are not given a choice to work or not work when you're on a farm during harvest time). I asked my mom and step-father for jobs around their house. I asked neighbors if they needed their driveways swept for a quarter, and so on. All throughout my childhood and teen years I was driven to work and have my own money. I enjoyed the independence and gratification it gave me to be able to buy things with my own money, like grown-ups. I was the only one of my friends who had a five-band radio, a television, a stereo and a tape recorder all in his own room back in the 60s; and I bought all of those items with my own money.

Well, in addition to my drive for business, my parent's divorce really set me back (in my adult years I was to learn that divorce has this same effect on almost all kids, but you don't know those things as a kid growing up). The impact of my parent's divorce is why I was also driven to better understand human emotion which led to my interest in the social-sciences. It was while I was in my 20s that I was able to piece things together for myself and make some major strides in my own personal development. This was when I discovered the cause-and-effect, and therefore the predictability of human emotions and their resulting behaviors. By my early 30s, I found myself with a duel drive to do business and implement in others the be-havioral tools and ideas I'd discovered in the social-sciences in my 20s. Thus, our counseling center was born in the mid-80s. On the surface, it seems like an odd paring; business drive and a social-sciences drive. However, who could have fore-seen where these two forces would have taken me? I certainly never could have.

What did your first boss teach you?
There are two different answers here. My first boss was both my dad and my grandfather as they farmed together after my parent's divorce. So, working in those fields, they always taught me to be responsible, do the job right the first time, and to not be lazy, putting off what needs to be done today.

My boss in my first "real" job (as an official employee at age 15-16) taught me to treat everyone with equal respect and equal opportunity. He was a gas-station owner and his son and I worked the station on the weekends, just the two of us. The owner favored his son over me (for obvious reasons). However, his son was lazy and unethical, always cutting corners, always just sitting around while I did most of the work when his dad was gone. I was the one who was expected to service customers while he sat inside the air-conditioned office watching television or listening to the radio.

When his dad was around, it was a different story. This kid would pick it up a bit, but he still played on his dad's favoritism. He'd take liberties in front of his dad that I or anyone else would get fired for. I would work extremely hard, get customer praises mentioned to the owner, but receive *no* recognition from the owner what-so-ever. His son would barely do his job, if that, and received constant praise and favors from his dad. That whole experience taught me about fairness and respect. Injustice and hardship are great teachers when we allow them to be.

What did working at such a young age teach you?
That work is fun and that I am happier when I am productive, accomplishing and serving others.

You've had a lot of success. Have you ever experienced rejection or failure in business?

Oh yes, several times and what it taught me was that most fail because they either quit or run out of resources. When I started my very first enterprise, KC-MAC, I went around to every potential customer at Kansas City's Municipal Airport, introducing myself and discussing their needs. Dozens of potential customers were telling me that they needed our service and they'd be using me then and there if we were already open for business.

Well, our grand-opening came and went and there was *no* business to be found. That was a mind-numbing experience. In the following months I went around to many of those same folks I'd talked with, some at length, just months before and all, to a person, acted as if they'd never met me. That was even more mind-numbing, especially with start-up business overhead and a family to feed staring me in the face. Pressure is the mother of invention. So, I set out to dig up customers. I could write a book on everything I did and experienced the first year to get that company off the ground. But after a year, it was not only going, but growing and rapidly. A few years later we were able to sell it for a handsome gain. But it never would have happened if not for all I learned from those initial rejections.

You've launched a leading-edge concept with Training-over-Time™. Are there any other innovations you are currently working on?

Yes, The ADAM Change Map™. Our ADAM Change Map ia a highly effective change management tool that continously provides us with the proven results our clients demand.

I once heard that the social-sciences aspect of your career started with teenagers. Are you currently doing anything with youth today?

Yes, we are in the early stages of developing a program aimed at youth who are not fortunate enough to be exposed to the academic and business ideas that others have; sort of like a YPO for *future* young presidents. I was one of those in a way. About 10 years ago, I met and formed a friendship with Norman Brinker; the Founder of restaurants like Steak & Ale, Chili's, and Macaroni Grill and the Father of casual dining. I remember often thinking, *"If only I'd met him when I was 20 years younger."*

Well, I know there are a lot of kids out there who, if given the opportunity, would and will be great men and women of business and contributors in society, if only they are exposed to the many and varied opportunities available in the world of business; M&As, Start-ups, V.C.s, Multi-conglomerates, etc. Most executives do not realize how fortunate they are to have had exposure to family who were university or even Ivy-league educated, or exposure to university educated peers, or exposure to Fortune 500 organizations, etc., while in their younger years.

If you are a kid who's exposure is limited to families and parents who drop out of school, or substance addictions, or where no one in your life-circle can see no real value to a college degree, much less an MBA or a top-tier university education, then you may very well miss out on the very life and opportunity that would fulfill and gratify your life. Unless you have some type of connections and/or exposure to *all* that this world as to offer in the world of business (and that does not happen through mainstream media) you will miss out on opportunities that could be the most fulfilling and life-rewarding. We're just wanting to do our part for some of those kids.

What did you learn in your undergraduate and graduate classes that turned out to be useful?

In college I majored in history and I am so glad I did. One can learn so much about both business and human behavior when you study history; actual events that transpired versus theories. Being analytical, my mind was always asking "why" to the historical events I was learning about; "why did they do this, or why do they do that?" It served as a platform for the further development of my problem-solving skills which I rely on extensively in my work with customer/clients today.

From both my undergrad and graduate work I learned three primary disciplines. First, the ability to make yourself remain focused. I cannot begin to tell you how often it seemed that those professors could have taken just 5-15 minutes to say what they said in 60 minutes. The temptation to dose off, doodle or be distracted is/was very real. You had to learn to create little mental devices, tools, systems to stay focused and alert with what the professor was teaching, because just as soon as you were not listening, they'd say something that would end up on an exam.

The second discipline I captured from my graduate studies was the use of the Greek language. From the Greek, I learned about the precision of communication. The English language is so imprecise and therefore rote with vagaries that cause so many communication breakdowns and problems in business and interpersonal communication. As long as the English language is the language of choice in world-wide business interactions we will continue to experience this very real problem within our enterprises. Some of the tools we've developed have been specifically designed to limit and restrict the faulty assumptions and vagaries that come with the English language.

A third benefit from my education was that I became a voracious reader. I did not grow up in a family that promoted reading. I watched a lot of television as a kid. Today, I read anywhere between 5 and 50 books a year depending on the year and the need.

When you started your first business, how did you approach leading and managing your employees?

I am a hands-off manager. I love working with a team or group of people and through the years, those I've worked with seem to have enjoyed the experience or so I've heard. We first identify their role and responsibilities and then my role is that of a manager/motivator to our people while I focus on the more strategic issues. I do not like to micro-manage people. Therefore, it has always been essential for me to get the right people working with me and around me on the front end; people who are responsible, intelligent, take initiative and who manage their responsibilities as if it were their own business.

Over the years, I have always been very fortunate to have some great people to work with and around me. That has been a major key to any success I've experienced.

What do you look for when you are considering taking on an organization as a client/customer?

Several things:

First *compatibility*; will we work together well? We work to figure this out during the initial interview phase. It's a business partnership. So, it is essential for us to be aligned in key areas.

Second, *character* and ethics. We have to be aligned about honesty, ethics and character. If we are not, then it is a pass for me.

Third, the *challenge*; is the project do-able and challenging? If so, it's a go for me and I hope for the potential customer/client as well.

You've been serving and partnering with companies for years. What do you think makes a consulting/training partnership work well?

Those three items I just list in the above question.

With such an intense job, how do you balance work and family?

Well, I am now fortunate enough to have all of my kids grown and on their own. Obviously, that wasn't the case for many years. In those days, frankly my business suffered as I made family my priority. Over the years, I'd seen far too many family-train-wrecks with clients and their families and so I worked hard to avoid that scenario. Now, I have much more freedom to devote myself to business and serving my customers. It is an exciting time for me.

You are well-known for being results-driven and analytical in a discipline that isn't known for objective data.

Right. I love seeing a person change and transform before my very eyes. That's exciting. And I am privileged to have been witness to this feat thousands of times spanning a couple of decades now.

How do you advise or coach executives on when to abandon a faulty plan and listen to their gut?

Early on. One of the first skills we impart is the ability to exert emotional self-control. Most executives are unaware of how much or to what extent their emotions affect their thinking and decision-making. When I first began advising and coaching business executives I was surprised to discover the extent to which most of them are influenced by their emotions. Though few would ever admit to such, but I think that is so because most are not even aware of how much influence their emotions have on their reasoning skills.

What people don't understand is that the more emotionally led or controlled you are, the more vulnerable and susceptible you will be to:

1. Being misled, by your own reasoning and/or by others,
2. Being taken advantage of by others of less than desirable character who know how to manipulate,
3. Making fatal business and/or personnel decisions.

So, early on in our performance development training we start the executive on a skills development path that:

- Controls emotion and its influence and impact on the psyche,
- Incorporates one's intuition or "gut,"
- Helps them know and experience the difference between "gut" and emotion because there is a difference and it is significant.

When you are working with an executive and you see them losing focus, how do you get them back on track?
Leverage. I find the leverage points within the individual. When or if we have to, I rely on these leverage points to help the trainee stay on track, stay the course until the process is complete. The trainee is the one who reaps most of the full benefit when she or he stays on track.

How do you change your approach from consulting with an executive of a Fortune 500 company to working with a small business start-up entrepreneur, and vice-versa?
It's not a matter of changing one's approach as much as it is an issue of experience and exposure. The effective coach-trainer-developer, must be proficient in the area or areas from which their clientele come from. While there are basic dynamics that are cross-functional, such as communication skills, leadership skills, delegation skills, etc., there are other dynamics that are particular to each trainee's background. With a Fortune 500 executive it might be the ability to have greater political awareness or corporate strategy awareness or company culture awareness. While with a start-up small business entrepreneur the more pressing dynamics might be investor awareness or direct-customer awareness. What helps me is my experience and exposure to both ends of this business spectrum/conundrum, allowing me to first, better understand and then second, better serve the needs and solutions that best fit my customers.

When you go in to a turnaround situation, how do you go about setting your own direction?
I do not and cannot set *my* direction. My job is to find *their* direction; what best fits them, within the perimeters of their corporate culture and structure. Then, it is my responsibility to walk my client through the process of first, removing the issues and obstacles hindering their success and then second, reclaiming their true direction and course of action. The answers to each one's (organization, team or individual) success typically lie within. They just need an experienced, objective, external influence to assist them out of where they are and into where they need to or should be.

What challenges come with being one of the most successful coach/trainer/consultants in business?
The skepticism of executives before they buy. Regardless of past successes, it is so obvious most have been burned in the past by or heard war-stories about consultants/trainers/coaches who did not deliver for one reason or another. The lost time and effect on morale in these situations is sometimes for more harmful than the lost expense. These past experiences tend to color a customer's objectivity, for totally understandable reasons too.

Life and business would be far better and far easier if people (outside consultants, coaches, trainers) would just be who they say they are and do what they say they will do. However, in the world in which we live, that simply is not the case anymore. So, it hinders those of us who are people of our word. On-the-other-hand, once our work begins, typically within just a few weeks (4-8 at the most) critical decision-makers are able to witness some positive impact results. From there, they tend to relax and trust in our process and the tools.

What are your passions?
Witnessing transformative behavior and change, both individual and team. It really ignites and excites me to see an individual, a team, or an organization just simply do the work, execute on the tools and then see them change and transform right before my very eyes. That's exciting.

At the end of the day, I can think of no greater joy or gratification because I know that the individual's, or team's, or organization's quality of experience and life is about to forever change for the better. So, although it's about business performance improvements, there is another benefit; the gratification of long-term, changed lives.

Do you ever get bored?
Yes.

What Clients Say

Trainee Perspective
Sr. VP Trainee, Fortune 200 Co.

"By the time you read this, our last session will have ended. As great as you are in your profession, I could not conceive departing without a few last words. I cannot speak any more highly of you professionally as I would have done at the end of our last session together. You remain "Top Shelf." It is more to you as a person and hopefully friend that I am thanking you today. You have had a chance to literally see me at my worse and at my best. I believe that is something that not all people get to experience together. I tell my wife often that you and I were scripted to meet long before my company was conceived. I am just not smart enough to speak to the ultimate purpose of these meetings. I can say I am a much better individual having met you. There are so many attributes I see in you that I can relate to and take pride in saying I know you. Thank you for this my friend. I could not leave you without a few of my favorite quotes that perhaps you can understand:

> *I have learned that success is to be measured not so much by the position that one has reached in life as by the obstacles which he has overcome while trying to succeed.*
> Booker T. Washington

> *The friend during my adversity I shall always cherish most. I can better trust those who helped to relieve the gloom of my dark hours than those who are so ready to enjoy with me the sunshine of my prosperity.*
> Ulysses S. Grant

> *Friendship is a strong and habitual inclination in two persons to promote the good and happiness of one another.*
> EustaceBudgell

> *Friends are an aid to the young to guard them from error. To the elderly, to attend to their wants and to supplement their failing power of action;*
> *To those in the prime of life, to assist them to noble deeds*
> Aristotle

Senior Executive Perspective
CEO, Fortune 500 Co.

*"Yesterday I attended a company-wide meeting. Our marketing department was presenting their plans to the 180 or so executives in attendance. Of particular interest was a 30-minute segment led by N.T. She was superb in her poise, self-confidence and command of material. She glowed and her audience responded in kind. Afterward, I overheard several people commenting on how she stood out among all the speakers that day. Later I reflected on the difference your development training made on her professional life. She is but one in a **series** of managers who've had the benefit of working with you. Our CFO, Director of Marketing, Director of Accounting, VP of Sales, VP of Human Resources, and several Senior Brand Managers have all had their career paths **accelerated** and their futures **improved** by completing you development program. They are **all** making more valuable contributions to the success and growth of our company because of you. Thank you for sharing your talent with us. We have **all** benefited from our association with you."*

Trainee Perspective
Mid-level Manager Trainee, Mid-sized Co.

When I first heard that I was to be spending time with a Leadership Trainer/Coach all kinds of thoughts went through my head:

" Am I all washed up at my company?

- What have I done or not done that they think I need coaching?
- What will this guy be like?
- I don't need a shrink.
- I don't have time for this, life is too busy already."

I want to thank you for dispelling ALL of these things and making the past year such a valuable experience for me.

I have met a man who is truly a giant in his business and I perceive in his personal life as well.

You are one of those rare people in business who has compassion and the experience to make me and others see a lot of things in ourselves; our surroundings, that we can change or adapt to in order to be better at our jobs and in our personal/family lives. I now have a lot of tools, knowledge and information that I did not have before. I am a tool guy, tools for working on material objects. So, your tools concept really works for me. I now have a clear business roadmap for my business future and I cannot thank you enough for everything you have done. This has truly been a rewarding experience. For all of this and many other things...A GREAT BIG THANK YOU! May God bless you and your business and family.

Senior Executive Perspective
CEO, Fortune 200 Co.

"Kevin, you helped us through a very delicate situation. You were able to align everyone's interests on a moving-forward basis; the shareholders, our Board, the outgoing CFO, and our executive team. I do not understand how you were able to do it, but you did it extremely well"

Trainee Perspective
Regional VP Trainee, Mid-sized Co.

"How do you thank a teacher and mentor for their priceless gift?
I will start by pledging to continue on with my growth and development.
I will do what I can to apply your training to reach my fullest potential.
Our time together will be documented by historians as the beginning of the executive phase of my career.

You are the third person to come along in my career that saw potential in me that others did not. All of you helped me to see it better, and challenged me to change my course. Each time in the past, this was followed by a long stretch of great opportunity and prosperity. So, my future is bright!
Self-awareness provides a calm confidence, and a real platform to operate as a leader and improve as a person. Thanks for helping me find it. Kevin, you are an exceptional, gifted person. I am proud to be a graduate of your executive training and coaching.

Thanks for me and my family. May God continue to bless you and your family.
Yours truly,
RM

"You cannot teach a man anything; you can only help him find it within himself." -- Galielo Galilei
"A teacher affects eternity; he can never tell where his influence stops."
-- Henry Adams

Senior Executive Perspective
President, Fortune 100 Best Places to Work Co.

*"Kevin, thanks for the final follow-up. You have done wonders. We still have a long journey ahead, but you have been a **MAJOR** contributor in giving us the tools to succeed. Thank you for that.*

I am eagerly reading your new book. What a great piece of work! We often work so hard to change ourselves or others, not realizing that we haven't dealt with one of the deep emotions and drivers of life, FEAR. I am sure that your efforts with this book will bring positive changes to those that read and practice the tools and habits you teach.

Kevin, thanks again for all you have done for our company. We are proud to count you as a friend and ally."

Trainee Perspective
Senior VP Trainee, Mid-sized Co.

"It's been three years now since your executive training/development work with me and my team and I wanted to let you know about the things that have stayed with me after all this time.

First, *I am not sure I ever told you, but I went to one of those week long leadership programs after our time together. The program was one of those where you take a bunch of surveys; they survey your co-workers, subordinates, and boss. Then, they watch you interact in different situations for about a week. At the end of that time they take everything they know about you and give you this feedback on what is wrong, what is right, and what to do to fix it. They were right on with **what you and I discovered about me.** I still don't know what is more amazing; the fact that they figured me out in a week, or the fact that **you figured me out without all those surveys**.*

*But the biggest difference between your program and theirs is that, even though I have a book, some notes and some contacts from that week in their program, **I still use your tools you gave me. What I learned from you and your tools has stayed with me much longer than anything else I have ever done.***

Second, *you have also worked with two of my highest financial performers (who also had some leadership issues). We have really been able to capitalize on the financial performance of some really dynamic producers without all of the "scorched earth" that sometimes comes with those types of personalities. At a company like ours, where you have to do two things: 1) be a servant leader, and 2) produce business results; your work has meant career growth and opportunity for those individuals as well as myself.*

Third, *when we were working together, it was at a low point in my professional career because of the results were were producing and the dynamics of our team. You were instrumental and key to helping me be more effective and the work you did was central to our extremely positive results (both **financial** and as it relates to **team** dynamics). The work that you have done for us has been going on for the past few years.*

I truly appreciate having your firm as a partner with us. You guys are ex-

tremely valuable to us as we continue to grow and get better at what we do. Thanks for all you do. I am eagerly reading your new book. What a great piece of work! We often work so hard to change ourselves or others, not realizing that we haven't dealt with one of the deep emotions and drivers of life, FEAR. I am sure that your efforts with this book will bring positive changes to those that read and practice the tools and habits you teach.

Kevin, thanks again for all you have done for our company. We are proud to count you as a friend and ally."

Thanks for all you do.

About TLS President
Kevin Turner

Kevin Turner's Unique Client Value

In the "profession" of *training*; executive development training and consulting, Kevin Turner is a businessman by experience, a minister by training, and an executive coach and trainer by passion. At the core, a minister is trained to understand and find clarity in the grey areas of decision-making, because as we all know, very few critical decisions are black & white, clear-cut, in and of themselves. It takes the ability to see beyond the immediate and calculate the down-the-road implications (2nd, 3rd, and even 4th impacts) of a given decision. Kevin's training (minister), coupled with his experience (businessman), gives him a unique ability to deliver his passion (coaching and development) to the clients he serves.

In addition to this, Kevin's strong sense of responsibility in serving his client/customers led him to author and create his state-of-the-art human performance systems and tools for which he is known and recognized for today. **Kevin's strengths are:**

1. Sound pattern recognition,
2. Understanding 2nd ,3rd, and 4th impacts (of actions taken or to be taken),
3. Drawing analogies from other industries and experiences,
4. Rigorous understanding of the microeconomics (resource allocation decision-making), and
5. Extensive experience working with multiple, cross-functional organizations, divisions, and business units.

Kevin has over 30 years of experience in Human Performance Development and Technology, bringing a wealth of knowledge, experience and expertise to his clients. Kevin views his vocation as a profession, not just a business. His reputation comes from putting customer's interests first and always telling them the truth. Kevin graduated from college with his Bachelor's Degree in just 3 years versus the traditional four or today's five and 6 year plans. Kevin Turner achieved entrepreneurial success at an early age. He was the founder and president of KC-MAC, an aviation restoration products and services company, when he was 23. After KC-MACs successful start-up, Kevin successfully sold the enterprise to local buyers and moved to North

Texas to obtain his Master's Degree in divinity with an emphasis in behavioral psychology.

Kevin achieved executive position at an early age as well. While pursuing his Master's Degree he served as the youngest minister in what was at that time the Nation's largest Protestant church. Then, as President and Founder, building on both his executive and entrepreneurial backgrounds, in the late 1980s Kevin built a counseling center in Dallas, Texas, that became one of the premier businesses of its kind throughout the Nation.

It was in the 1990s that Kevin's unique "Tool" system of behavioral modification and human performance gained wide-spread popularity. Kevin's unique ability to create and craft tools and solutions around specific people problems that produce long-term, time-effective results garnered him nationwide attention with over 1,000 television, radio and print interviews. It was during this time that Kevin served as the Corporate Coach and Relationships Expert for television's NBC5 in Dallas from 1999 to 2003.

TLS Consulting and Leadership Development firm began as an off-shoot of the counseling center. A lot of business executives were coming to the center for personal and marriage issues and many would ask Kevin if he'd ever considered consulting and corporate coaching. Kevin finally said yes one day when a senior executive asked Kevin if he'd come and work with his company's National Sales Team in the late 90s. It was a Fortune 500, NASDAQ traded company. Since that time, Kevin has consulted, given keynotes and speeches, and trained executives for over 275 public and private companies from a wide-spectrum of industries. A list of the top fifty client organizations is available by going to TLS Customers Served

http://www.TLS-t3.com
(972) 233-9998
P.O. Box 2543| Addison, TX 75001

About Turner Leadership Strategies, Intl.

With offices at the same location for twenty-plus years, TLS is small enough to be flexible and responsive to your specific needs and concerns, large and capable enough to support your multi-state and international organization, and stable enough to serve you for years to come.

In addition to this, TLS is one of only a few consulting and human development firms in the industry to offer its clients a Written Guarantee, greatly reducing your risk of engagement.

TLS is an executive and organization consulting and development firm specializing in helping companies build strong management executives and teams that meet the competitive needs of today's competitive business environment.

Operating in Dallas, Texas since 1986, TLS and its parent LICS service client/customers throughout the continental US, Canada, Europe and abroad. TLS has worked with both private and public sector organizations from small business start-ups to Fortune 500 Companies as a consultant, coach, and professional advisor.

TLS is an innovative management consulting firm that leaders trust to provide specialized and cross-functional expertise in delivery of low-risk solutions and lasting results. With hundreds of successful engagements across both public and private sectors, our experience and exposure gives us the flexibility and responsiveness of a small business, along with the reach and strength of a much larger organization. Powered by our commitment to our client/customers, we embrace our client's mission as our own.

TLS is committed to providing our customers with practical, time-effective, results-based performance development programs and tools.

Fundamental to this philosophy is insuring that each of our engagements provides the individual and the organization with the ability to achieve measurable goals and objectives. Furthermore, these engagements must provide the opportunity to develop skills and abilities that improve the individual and organizational performance. Experience tells us that skills will be adopted and performance improved only when the participant sees how these skills apply to his world of influence. For change to occur, theory must be translated into practical reality.

Bibliography - by Author

Alessandra, Tony, Ph.d., Phil Wexler, and Rick Barrera. *Non-Manipulative Selling: Strategies & Techniques for Creating Customers, Not Just Sales.* New York: Prentice Hall Press, 1987.

Ariely, Dan. *Predictably Irrational: The Hidden Forces That Shape Our Decisions.* New York: Harper Perennial, 2008.

Autry, James A. *The Servant Leader: How to Build a Creative Team, Develop Great Morale, and Improve Bottome-Line Performance.* Roseville, CA: Prima Publishing, 2001.

Baldrige, Letitia. *Lititia Baldrige's New Complete Guide to Executive Manners.* New York: Rawson Associates, 1985, 1993.

Battlle, John. *The Search: How Google and Its Rivals Rewrote the Rules of Business and Transformed our Culture.* New York: Penguin Books, 2005.

Beatty, Jack. *Colossus: How the Corporation Changed America.* New York: Broadway Books, 2001.

BenDaniel, David J., and Arthur H. Rosenbloom. *Doing the Deal: International M&A Joint Ventures & Beyond.* New York: John Wiley & Sons, 1998.

Bennis, Warren, Daniel Goleman, and James O'Toole. *Transparency: How Leaders Create a Culture of Candor.* San Francisco: Jossey-Bass, 2008.

Bennis, Warren, and Noel M. Tichey. *Judgment: How Winning Leaders Make Great Calls.* New York: Pennguin Group, 2007.

Begley, Sharon. *Train Your Mind, Change Your Brain.* New York: Ballantine Books, 2008.

Bettger, Frank. *How I Raised Myself from Failure to Success in Selling.* New York: Simon & Schuster, 1949.

Blanchard, Ken, and Phil Hodges. *The Servant Leader: Transforming Your Heart, Head, Hands, and Habits.* Nashville, TN: Thomas Nelson, Inc., 2003.

Blanchard, Ken, and John Britt. *Who Killed Change?: Solving the Mystery of Leading People Through Change*. New York: William Morrow; An Imprint of HarperCollins, 2009.

Bossidy, Larry, and Ram Charan. *Confronting Reality: Doing What Matters to Get Things Right*. New York: Crowne Business Books, 2004.

Boston Consulting Group. *On Strategy: Cash Cows, Experience Curves, Time-Based Competition, Richness and Reach, and Other BCG Ideas*. New York: John Wiley & Sons, 2006.

Bower, Marvin. *The Will to Lead: Running a Business with a Network of Leaders*. Boston, MA: Harvard Business school Press, 1997.

Bower, Marvin. *The Will to Manage: Corporate Success Through Programmed Management*. New York: McGraw-Hill, 1966.

Boylan, Michael A. *Accelerants: 12 Strategies to Sell Faster, Close Deals Faster, and Grow Business Faster*. New York: Penguin Group, 2007.

Brafman, Ori, and Rom Brafman. *Sway: The Irresistible Pull of Irrational Behavior*. New York: Double Day, 2008.

Brem, Marion Luna. *Women Make the Best Salesmen*. New York: Double Day, 2004.

Brinker, Norman, and Donald T. Phillips. *On The Brink: The Life and Leadership of Norman Brinker*. Texas: Summit, 1996.

Brodsky, Norm, and Bo Burlingham. *The Knack: How Street-Smart Entrepreneurs Learn to Handle Whatever Comes Up*. New York: Penguin Group, 2008.

Brooks, David. *The Social Animal: The Hidden Sources of Love, Character, and Achievement*. New York: Random House, 2011.

Brett, Jeanne. *Negotiating Globally: How to Negotiate Deals, Resolve Disputes, and Make Decisions Across Cultural Boundaries*. San Francisco: Jossey-Bass, 2007.

Buckingham, Marcus, and Donald O. Clifton, Ph.D. Now, Discover Your Strengths. New York: The Free Press – Simon & Schuster, 2001.

Cain, Gordon. *Everybody Wins!: A Life in Free Enterprise*. Philadelphia: Chemical Heritage Press, 2001.

Camp, Jim. *Start with No*. New York: Crowne Publishing, 2002.

Cannadine, David. *Mellon: An American Life*. New York: Alfred A. Knopf, 2006.

Carnegie, Andrew. *The Autobiography of Andrew Carnegie*. New York: Penguin Group, 2006.

Carnegie, Dale. *Effective Speaking: The Quick and Easy Way*. New York: Dale Carnegie & Associates, 1962.

Carnegie, Dale. *How to Win Friends & Influence People*. New York: Simon & Schuster, 1936, 1964.

Carroll, Paul B., and Chunka Mui. *Billion Dollar Lessons: What Your can Learn from the Most Inexcusable Business Failures of the Last 25 Years*. New York: Penguin Group, 2008, 2009.

Casperson, Dana May. *Power Etiquette: What You Don't Know Can Kill Your Career*. New York: AMACOM, American Management Association, 1999.

Chernow, Ron. *The House of Morgan: An American Banking Dynasty and the Rise of Modern Finance*. New York: Atlantic Monthly Press, 1990.

Cialdini, Robert B. Ph.D. *Influence: The Psychology of Persuasion*. New York: Quill, 1984, 1993.

Charan, Ram, Stephen Drotter, and James Noel. *The Leadership Pipeline: How to Build the Leadership-Powered Company*. New York: Jossey-Bass, A John Wiley Company, 2001.

Cohen, Allan R., and David L. Bradford. *Influence without Authority: The Way to Get Things Done at Work*. New York: John Wiley & Sons, 1989, 1991.

Collins, Jim, and Jerry I. Porras. *Built to Last: Successful Habits of Visionary Companies*. New York: HarperCollins, 1994.

Collins, Jim. *Good to Great: Why Some Companies Make the Leap – and Others Don't*. New York: HarperCollins, 2001.

Colvin, Geoff. *Talent is Overrated: What Really Separates World-Class Performers from Everybody Else*. New York: Penguin Books, 2008.

Covey, Stephen R. *The 7 Habits of Highly Effective People*. New York:

Simon & Schuster, 1989.

Cozolino, Louis. *The Neuroscience of Human Relationships: Attachment and the Developing Social Brain*. New York: W.W. Norton & Co., 2006.

Csikszentmihalyi, Mihaly. *Flow: The Psychology of Optimal Experience*. New York: Harper Perennial Modern Classics, 2008.

Dispenza, Joe D.C. *Evolve the Brain: The Science of Changing Your Mind*. Deerfield Beach, Florida, 2007.

Doidge, Norman. *The Brain That Changes Itself*. New York: Penguin, 2007.

Ellis, Joseph J. *Founding Brothers: The Revolutionary Generation*. New York: Vintage Books, 2000

Eccles, Robert G., and Dwight B. Crane. *Doing Deals: Investment Banks at Work*. Boston, MA: Harvard Business Press, 1988.

Edersheim, Elizabeth Haas. *McKinsey's Marvin Bower: Vision, Leadership & the Creation of Management Consulting*. New York: John Wiley & Sons, 2004.

Ehrlich, Paul R. *Human Natures: Genes, Cultures, and the Human Prospect*. New York: Penguin Books, 2000.

Ferrazzi, Keith. *Who's Got Your Back: The Breakthrough Program to Build Deep, Trusting Relationships that Create Success – And Won't Let You Fail*. New York: Broadway Books, 2009.

Finkelstein, Sydney. *Why Smart Executives Fail: And What You Can Learn from Their Mistakes*. New York: Penguin Portfolio Trade, 2004.

Fischer, Peter. *The New Boss: How to Survive the First 100 Days*. London: Kogan-Page, 2007.

Fisher, Roger, William L. Ury, and Bruce Patton. *Getting to Yes: Negotiating Agreement Without Giving In*. New York: Penguin, 1991.

Fishman, Charles. *The Wal-Mart Effect: How the World's Most Powerful Company Really Works – And How It's Transforming the American Economy*. New York: Penguin Press, 2006.

Fraser, Steve. *Every Man a Speculator: A History of Wall Street in American Life*. New York: HarperCollins Publishers, 2005.

Freese, Thomas A. *Secrets of Question-Based Selling: How the Most Pow-

erful Tool in Business Can Double Your Sales Results. Naperville, IL: Sourcebooks, Inc., 2000, 2003.

Freiberg, Kevin, and Jackie Freiberg. *Nuts! Southwest Airlines' Crazy Recipe for Business and Personal Success.* New York: Random House Broadway Books, 1998.

Friga, Paul N. Ph.D. *The McKinsey Engagement: A Powerful Toolkit for more Efficient & Effective Team Problem Solving.* New York: McGraw-Hill, 2009.

Frishman, Rick, and Jill Lublin. *Networking Magic: Finding the Best.* Avon, MA: Adams Media, 2004.

Frith, Chris. *Making Up The Mind: How the Brain Creates Our Mental World.* Maldon, MA: Blackwell, 2008.

Fuqua, J.B. *Fuqua: How I Made My Fortune Using Other People's Money.* Atlanta: Longstreet Press, 2001.

Gerstner, Louis V. Jr. *Who Says Elephants Can't Dance: Leading a Great Enterprise Through Dramatic Change.* New York: HarperCollins, 2002.

Gladwell, Malcolm. *Blink: The Power of Thinking Without Thinking.* Boston: Little, Brown, and Company, 2005.

Gladwell, Malcolm. *Outliers: The Story of Success.* Boston: Little, Brown, and Company, 2008.

Gladwell, Malcolm. *The Tipping Point: How Little Things Can Make a Big Difference.* Boston: Little, Brown, and Company, 2000.

Godin, Seth. *Tribes: We Need You to Lead Us.* New York: The Penguin Group; Portfolio, 2008.

Goleman, Daniel. *Emotional Intelligence: Why It Can Matter More Than IQ.* New York: Bantom Books, 2006.

Goldstein, Leonard, Timothy Nolan, and J. William Pfeiffer. *Applied Strategic Planning: How to Develop a Plan That Really Works.* New York: McGraw-Hill, 1993.

Gordon, John Steele. *An Empire of Wealth: The Epic History of American Economic Power.* New York: HarperCollins Publishers, 2004.

Greenberg, Herb, Harold Weinstein, and Patrick Sweeney. *How to Hire &*

Develop Your Next Your Next Top Performer: The Five Qualities That Make Salespeople Great. New York: McGraw-Hill, 2001.

Gubman, Edward L. *The Talent Solution: Aligning Strategy and People to Achieve Extraordinary Results.* New York: McGraw-Hill, 1998.

Hammer, Michael, and James Champy. *Reengineering the Corporation: A Manifesto for Business Revolution.* New York: HarperCollins, 1993.

Harding, Ford. *Creating Rainmakers: The Manager's Guide to Training Professionals to Attract New Clients.* New York: John Wiley & Sons, 2006.

Harding, Ford. *Rain-Making: Attracting New Clients.* Holbrook, MA: Adams Media Corp., 1994.

Harman, Sidney. *Mind Your Own Business: A Maverick's Guide to Business, Leadership and Life.* New York: Double Day, 2003.

Harvard Business Review. *Change: Harvard Business Review on Change.* Cambridge, MA: Harvard Business School Press, 1991, 1993, 1995, 1996, 1997, 1998.

Heath, Chip, and Dan Heath. *Switch: How to Change Things When Change is Hard.* New York: Broadway Books, 2010.

Hill, Napoleon. *Think and Grow Rich.* Greenwich, Conn: Fawcett Publications, 1937.

Hogan, Kevin. *The Secret Language of Business: How to Read Anyone in 3 Seconds or Less.* New York: John Wiley & Sons, 2008.

Hogan, Kevin. *The Science of Influence: How to Get Anyone to Say Yes in 8 minutes or Less!.* New York: John Wiley & Sons, 2005.

Hooke, Jeffrey C. *M&A: A Practical guide to Doing the Deal.* New York: John Wiley & Sons, 1997.

Hubbard, Douglas W. *How to Measure Anything: Finding the Value of "Intangibles" in Business.* New York: John Wiley & Sons, 2010.

Iacoboni, Marco. *Mirroring People: The New Science of How We Connect with Others.* New York: Farrar, Straus, and Giroux, 2008.

Isaacson, Walter. *Benjamin Franklin: An American Life.* New York: Simon & Schuster, 2003.

Johnson, Paul E.. *A Shopkeeper's Millennium: Society and Revival in Rochester, New York, 1815-1837.* New York: Hill and Wang, 1978, 2004.

Kadlec, Daniel J. *Masters of The Universe: Winning Strategies of America's
Greatest Dealmakers.* New York: Harper Collins Publishers, 1999.

Kanter, Rosabeth Moss. *Confidence: How Winning Streaks & Losing
Streaks Begin & End.* New York: Crowne Business, 2004.

Kaplan, Justin. *When the Astors Owned New York: Blue Bloods and Grand
Hotels in a Gilded Age.* New York: Viking Penguin, 2006.

Kawasaki, Guy. *Reality Check: The Irreverent Guide to Outsmarting,
Outmanaging, and Ourmarketing Your Competition.* New York: Penguin
Group, 2008.

Kawasaki, Guy. *The Art of The Start: Time-Tested, Battle-Hardened Guide
for Anyone Starting Anything.* New York: Penguin Group, 2004.

Kiechel, Walter, III. *The Lords of Strategy: The Secret Intellectual History
of the New Corporate World.* Boston, MA: Harvard Business School
Press, 2010.

Klein, Gary. *The Power of Intuition.* New York: Doubleday, 2003.

Klingberg, TZorkel. *The Overflowing Brain: Information Overload and the
Limits of Working Memory.* New York: Oxford University Press, 2009.

Kotkin, Joel. *Tribes: How Race, Religion, and Identity Determine Success
in the Global Economy.* New York: Random House, 1992,

Kotter, John P. *Power and Influence: Beyond Formal Authority.* New York:
The Free Press, a Division of McMillan, 1985.

Laird, Pamela Walker. *Pull: Networking and Success since Benjamin Franklin.* Cambridge, MA: Harvard University Press.

Lajoux, Alexandra Reed. *The Art of M&A Integration: A Guide to Merging
Resources, Processes & Responsibilities.* New York: McGraw-Hill 2006.

Lawrence, Paul R. and Nitin Nohria. *Driven: How Human Nature Shapes
our Choices.* New York: Jossey-Bass, 2002.

Leeds, Dorothy. *The 7 Powers of Questions: Secrets to Successful Communication in Life and at Work.* New York: Penguin Group, 2000.

Levitt, Steven D., and Stephen J. Dubner. *Freakonomics: A Rogue Economist Explores The Hidden Side of Everything.* New York: HarperCollins, 2005.

Libet, Benjamin. *Mind Time: The Temporal Factor in Consciousness.* Cambridge, MA: Harvard University Press, 2004.

Lieberman, David J. Ph.D. *Get Anyone to do Anything and Never Feel Powerless Again.* New York: St. Martin's Griffin, 2000.

Lindstrom, Martin. *Buy-ology: Truth and Lies About Why We Buy.* New York: Double Day, 2008.

Lombardi, Vince Jr. *What It Takes to be #1: Vince Lombardi on Leadership.* New York: McGraw-Hill, 2001.

MacKay, Harvey. *Swim With the Sharks.* New York: William Morrow, 1988.

Magee, David. *Turnaround: How Carlos Ghosn Rescued Nissan.* New York: HarperCollins, 2003.

Marcus, James. *Amazonia: Five Years at the Epicenter of the Dot.Com Juggernaut.* New York: The New Press, 2005.

McCullough, David. *1776.* New York: Simon & Schuster, 2005.

McGarvie, Blythe. *Fit In Stand Out: The Key to Leadership Effectiveness in Business and Life.* New York: McGraw-Hill, 2006.

McQueen, Rod. *Blackberry: The Inside Story of Research In Motion.* Toronto, Ontario, Canada: Key Porter Books, 2010.

Miller, Robert B., and Stephen E. Heiman. *Strategic Selling: The Unique Sales System Proven Successful by America's Best Companies.* New York: Warner Books, 1985.

Miller, Robert B., and Stephen E. Heiman. *The New Strategic Selling: The Unique Sales System Proven Successful by America's Best Companies.* New York: Warner Books, 1998.

Miller, Steve. *The Turnaround Kid: What I Learned Rescuing America's Most Troubled Companies.* New York: HarperCollins, 2008.

Mitchell, Jack. *Hug Your Customers: The Proven Way to Personalize Sales and Achieve Astounding Results.* New York: Hyperion, 2003.

Mitchell, Jack. *Hug Your People: The Proven Way to Hire, Inspire, and Recognize Your Employees and Achieve Remarkable Results.* New York: Hyperion, 2008.

Mlodinow, Leonard. *The Drunkard's Walk: How Randomness Rules Our Lives.* New York: Pantheon Books, 2008.

Monarth, Harrison. *Executive Presence: The Art of Commanding Respect Like a CEO.* New York: McGraw-Hill, 2010.

Montague, Read. *Why Choose This Book?: How to Make Decisions.* London: Dutton, 2006.

Murray, David Kord. *Borrowing Brilliance: The Six Steps to Business Innovation by Building on the Ideas of Others.* New York: Gotham Press & Penguin Books, 2009.

Nasaw, David. Andrew Carnegie. New York: Penguin Press, 2006.

Pfeffer, Jeffrey, and O'Reilly, Charles A. III. *Hidden Value: How Great Companies Achieve Extraordinary Results with Ordinary People.* Boston, MA: Harvard Business School Press, 2000.

Pachter, Barbara. *When the Little Things Count . . . And They Always Count: 601 Essential Things That Everyone in Business Needs to Know.* New York: Marlowe & Co., 2001, 2006.

Parkhurst, William. *The Eloquent Executive: A Guide to High-Impact Speaking in Big Meetings, Small Meetings, and One-on-One.* New York: Times Books, 1988.

Parinello, Anthony. *Think and Sell Like a CEO.* Canada: Entrepreneur Press, 2002.

Patterson, Kerry, Joseph Grenny, David Maxfield, Ron McMillan, and Al Switzler. *Influencer: The Power to Change Anything.* New York: McGraw-Hill, 2008.

Paul, Marla. *The Friendship Crisis: Finding, Making, and Keeping Friends When You're Not a Kid Anymore.* Emmaus, Pennsylvania: Rodale Press, 2004.

Pfeffer, Jeffrey. *Power: Why Some People Have it – and Others Don't.* New York: HarperCollins, 2010.

Pfeffer, Jeffrey. *The Human Equation: Building Profits by Putting People*

First. Boston, MA: Harvard Business School Press, 1998.

Pfeffer, Jeffrey, and Robert I. Sutton. *The Knowing-Doing Gap: How Smart Companies Turn Knowledge into Action.* Boston, MA: Harvard Business School Press, 2000.

Phillips, Donald T. *The Founding Fathers on Leadership: Classic Teamwork in Changing Times.* New York: Warner Books, 1997.

Phillips, Donald T. *Lincoln on Leadership: Executive Strategies for Tough Times.* New York: Warner Books, 1993.

Phillips, Jack J. Ph.D., and Ron Drewstone. *How to Measure Training Results: The Practical Guide to Tracking the Six Key Indicators.* New York: McGraw-Hill, 2002.

Phillips, Jack J. Ph.D., Timothy W. Bothell, Ph.D., and G. Lynne Snead. *Crucial Confrontations: Tools for Resolving Broken Promises, Violated Expectations, and Bad Behavior.* New York: McGraw-Hill, 2005.

Phillips, Jack J. Ph.D., Timothy W. Bothell, Ph.D., and G. Lynne Snead. *The Project Management Scorecard: Measuring the Success of Project Management Solutions.* New York: Butterworth-Heinemann, 2002.

Porter, Eduardo. *The Price of Everything: Solving the Mystery of Why We Pay What We Do.* London: Penguin Books, 2011.

Porter, Michael E. *Competitive Strategy: Techniques for Analyzing Industries and Competitors.* New York: The Free Press, a Division of MacMillan Publishing Company, 1980.

Porter, Michael E. *On Competition.* Boston, MA: Harvard Business Review Book, 1998.

Porter, Michael E., Cynthia A. Montgomery, and Harvard Business Review. *Strategy: Seeking and Securing Competitive Advantage.* Boston, MA: Harvard Business School Press, 1979, 1980, 1981, 1983-1991.

Rackham, Neil. *Major Account Sales Strategy.* New York: McGraw-Hill, 1989.

Rackham, Neil, and John DeVincentis. *Rethinking the Sales Force: Redefining Selling to Create and Capture Customer Value.* New York" McGraw-Hill, 1999.

Rackham, Neil. *Spin Selling.* New York: McGraw-Hill, 1988.

Rasiel, Ethan M. *The McKinsey Way: Using the Techniques of the World's Top Strategic Consultants to Help You and Your Business.* New York: McGraw-Hill, 1999.

Reichheld, Fred. The Ultimate Question: Driving Good Profits and True Growth. Boston, MA: Harvard Business School Press, 2006.

Renehan, Edward J. Jr. *Commodore: The Life of Cornelius Vanderbilt.* New York: Perseus Books Group, 2007.

Rickertsen, Rick. *Buyout: The Insider's Guide to Buying Your Own Company.* New York: AMACOM, American Management Association, 2001.

Robert, Michel. *Strategy: Pure & Simple.* New York: McGraw-Hill, 1993.

Robert, Michel. *The Power of Strategic Thinking: Lock in Markets, Lock Out Competitors.* New York: McGraw-Hill, 2000.

Rye, David E., and Craig R. Hickman. *Starting Up: Do You Have What it Takes to Make it in Your Own Business?* Paramus, NJ: Prentice Hall Press, 1997.

Schwartz, Barry. *The Paradox of Choice: Why More is Less.* New York: Harper Perennial, 2004.

Schwartz, Jeffrey, and Sharon Begley. *The Mind and the Brain: Neuroplasticity and the Power of Mental Force.* New York: Harper Perennnial, 2002.

Shapiro, Ronald M., and Mark A. Jankowski. *Bullies, Tyrants, and Impossible People.* New York: Crown Business, 2005.

Siegal, Daniel J. *The Developing Mind: How Relationships and the Brain Interact to Shape Who We Are.* New York: Guilford Press, 1999.

Simons, Tony. *The Integrity Dividend: Leading by The Power of Your Word.* New York: Jossey-Bass, 2008.

Slack, Charles. *Hetty: The Genius and Madness of America's First Female Tycoon.* New York: Harper Collins Publishers, 2004.

Smartt, Geoff, and Randy Street. *Who: Solve Your #1 Problem – Finding Who to Do It!.* New York: Ballantine Books, 2008.

Stanley, Thomas, J. Ph.D. *The Millionaire Mind.* Kansas City: Andrews McMeel Publishing, 2000.

Strouse, Jean. *Morgan: American Financier*. New York: Harper Perennial Publishers, 2000.

Surowiecki, James. *The Wisdom of Crowds: Why the Many are Smarter than the Few and How Collective Wisdom Shapes Business, Economies, Societies, and Nations*. New York: Doubleday, 2004.

Taleb, Nassim Nichloas. *The Black Swain: The Impact of the Highly Improbable*. New York: Random House, 2007.

Turner, Kevin. *Change is Good: Creating Opportunity Amidst Uncertainty*. Texas: Ashley Down Business Press, 2011.

Tutelman, Cary J., and Larry D. Hause. *The Balance Point: New Ways Business Owners Can Use Boards*. Edina, Minn.: Famillepress, 2008.

Ury, William. *Getting Past No: Negotiating with Difficult People*. New York: Bantam Books, 1991.

Van Hecke, Madeleine. *Blind Spots: Why Smart People Do Dumb Things*. Amherst, NY: Prometheus Books, 2007.

Van Hecke, Madeleine, Lisa P. Callahan, Brad Kolar, and Ken A. Paller. *The Brain Advantage: Become a More Effective Business Leader Using the Latest Brain Research*. Amherst, NY: Prometheus books, 2010.

Wall Street Journal. *The Wall Street Journal Book of Chief Executive Style: Amenities and Customs of America's Corporate Elite*. New York: William Morrow and Co., 1989.

Watts, Duncan J. *Six Degrees: The Science of a Connected Age*. New York: W.W. Norton, 2003.

Weissman, Jerry. *Presenting to Win: The Art of Telling Your Story*. Upper Saddle River, NJ: FT Press, 2006.

Whiteley, Richard C. *The Customer-Driven Company: Moving From Talk to Action*. Reading, MA: Perseus Books, 1991.

Wiseman, Liz. *Multipliers: How the Best Leaders Make Everyone Smarter*. New York: HarperCollins, 2010.

Wooden, John. *Wooden on Leadership*. New York: McGraw-Hill, 2005.

Wyly, Sam. *1,000 Dollars & An Idea: Entrepreneur to Billionaire*. New York: New Market Press, 2008.

Bibliography - By Topic

Brain Science & Business Psychology

Business

Change

Classics

Consulting

Executive Presence

History Business

Leadership

Networking

Sales & Development

Strategy

General

Brain Science & Business Psychology

Ariely, Dan. *Predictably Irrational: The Hidden Forces That Shape Our Decisions*. New York: Harper Perennial, 2008.

Begley, Sharon. *Train Your Mind, Change Your Brain*. New York: Ballantine Books, 2008.

Brafman, Ori, and Rom Brafman. *Sway: The Irresistible Pull of Irrational Behavior*. New York: Double Day, 2008.

Brooks, David. *The Social Animal: The Hidden Sources of Love, Character, and Achievement*. New York: Random House, 2011.

Cialdini, Robert B. Ph.D. *Influence: The Psychology of Persuasion*.

New York: Quill, 1984, 1993.

Colvin, Geoff. *Talent is Overrated: What Really Separates World-Class Performers from Everybody Else.* New York: Penguin Books, 2008.

Cozolino, Louis. *The Neuroscience of Human Relationships: Attachment and the Developing Social Brain.* New York: W.W. Norton & Co., 2006.

Csikszentmihalyi, Mihaly. *Flow: The Psychology of Optimal Experience.* New York: Harper Perennial Modern Classics, 2008.

Dispenza, Joe D.C. *Evolve the Brain: The Science of Changing Your Mind.* Deerfield Beach, Florida, 2007.

Doidge, Norman. *The Brain That Changes Itself.* New York: Penguin, 2007.

Ehrlich, Paul R. *Human Natures: Genes, Cultures, and the Human Prospect.* New York: Penguin Books, 2000.

Frith, Chris. *Making Up The Mind: How the Brain Creates Our Mental World.* Maldon, MA: Blackwell, 2008.

Goleman, Daniel. *Emotional Intelligence: Why It Can Matter More Than IQ.* New York: Bantom Books, 2006.

Hogan, Kevin. *The Secret Language of Business: How to Read Anyone in 3 Seconds or Less.* New York: John Wiley & Sons, 2008.

Iacoboni, Marco. *Mirroring People: The New Science of How We Connect with Others.* New York: Farrar, Straus, and Giroux, 2008.

Klein, Gary. *The Power of Intuition.* New York: Doubleday, 2003.

Klingberg, TZorkel. *The Overflowing Brain: Information Overload and the Limits of Working Memory.* New York: Oxford University Press, 2009.

Lawrence, Paul R. and Nitin Nohria. *Driven: How Human Nature Shapes our Choices.* New York: Jossey-Bass, 2002.

Levitt, Steven D., and Stephen J. Dubner. *Freakonomics: A Rogue Economist Explores The Hidden Side of Everything.* New York: HarperCollins, 2005.

Libet, Benjamin. *Mind Time: The Temporal Factor in Consciousness.* Cambridge, MA: Harvard University Press, 2004.

Lieberman, David J. Ph.D. *Get Anyone to do Anything and Never Feel Powerless Again.* New York: St. Martin's Griffin, 2000.

Lindstrom, Martin. *Buy-ology: Truth and Lies About Why We Buy.* New York: Double Day, 2008.

Montague, Read. *Why Choose This Book?: How to Make Decisions.* London: Dutton, 2006.

Porter, Eduardo. *The Price of Everything: Solving the Mystery of Why We Pay What We Do.* London: Penguin Books, 2011.

Schwartz, Barry. *The Paradox of Choice: Why More is Less.* New York: Harper Perennial, 2004.

Schwartz, Jeffrey, and Sharon Begley. *The Mind and the Brain: Neuroplasticity and the Power of Mental Force.* New York: Harper Perennnial, 2002.

Siegal, Daniel J. *The Developing Mind: How Relationships and the Brain Interact to Shape Who We Are.* New York: Guilford Press, 1999.

Stanley, Thomas, J. Ph.D. *The Millionaire Mind.* Kansas City: Andrews McMeel Publishing, 2000.

Surowiecki, James. *The Wisdom of Crowds: Why the Many are Smarter than the Few and How Collective Wisdom Shapes Business, Economies, Societies, and Nations.* New York: Doubleday, 2004.

Turner, Kevin. *Change is Good: Creating Opportunity Amidst Uncertainty.* Texas: Ashley Down Business Press, 2011.

Van Hecke, Madeleine. *Blind Spots: Why Smart People Do Dumb Things.* Amherst, NY: Prometheus Books, 2007.

Van Hecke, Madeleine, Lisa P. Callahan, Brad Kolar, and Ken A. Paller. *The Brain Advantage: Become a More Effective Business Leader Using the Latest Brain Research.* Amherst, NY: Prometheus books, 2010.

Business

Battlle, John. *The Search: How Google and Its Rivals Rewrote the Rules of Business and Transformed our Culture*. New York: Penguin Books, 2005.

Beatty, Jack. *Colossus: How the Corporation Changed America*. New York: Broadway Books, 2001.

Bennis, Warren, Daniel Goleman, and James O'Toole. *Transparency: How Leaders Create a Culture of Candor*. San Francisco: Jossey-Bass, 2008.

Bennis, Warren, and Noel M. Tichey. *Judgment: How Winning Leaders Make Great Calls*. New York: Pennguin Group, 2007.

Carroll, Paul B., and Chunka Mui. *Billion Dollar Lessons: What Your can Learn from the Most Inexcusable Business Failures of the Last 25 Years*. New York: Penguin Group, 2008, 2009.

Collins, Jim, and Jerry I. Porras. *Built to Last: Successful Habits of Visionary Companies*. New York: HarperCollins, 1994.

Collins, Jim. *Good to Great: Why Some Companies Make the Leap – and Others Don't*. New York: HarperCollins, 2001.

Fishman, Charles. *The Wal-Mart Effect: How the World's Most Powerful Company Really Works – And How It's Transforming the American Economy*. New York: Penguin Press, 2006.

Freiberg, Kevin, and Jackie Freiberg. *Nuts! Southwest Airlines' Crazy Recipe for Business and Personal Success*. New York: Random House Broadway Books, 1998.

Gladwell, Malcolm. *Blink: The Power of Thinking Without Thinking*. Boston: Little, Brown, and Company, 2005.

Gladwell, Malcolm. *Outliers: The Story of Success*. Boston: Little, Brown, and Company, 2008.

Gladwell, Malcolm. *The Tipping Point: How Little Things Can Make a Big Difference*. Boston: Little, Brown, and Company, 2000.

Hubbard, Douglas W. *How to Measure Anything: Finding the Value of*

"Intangibles" in Business. New York: John Wiley & Sons, 2010.

Kadlec, Daniel J. *Masters of The Universe: Winning Strategies of America's Greatest Dealmakers.* New York: Harper Collins Publishers, 1999.

Kanter, Rosabeth Moss. *Confidence: How Winning Streaks & Losing Streaks Begin & End.* New York: Crowne Business, 2004.

Kawasaki, Guy. *Reality Check: The Irreverent Guide to Outsmarting, Outmanaging, and Ourmarketing Your Competition.* New York: Penguin Group, 2008.

Kotkin, Joel. *Tribes: How Race, Religion, and Identity Determine Success in the Global Economy.* New York: Random House, 1992,

Marcus, James. *Amazonia: Five Years at the Epicenter of the Dot. Com Juggernaut.* New York: The New Press, 2005.

McQueen, Rod. *Blackberry: The Inside Story of Research In Motion.* Toronto, Ontario, Canada: Key Porter Books, 2010.

Murray, David Kord. *Borrowing Brilliance: The Six Steps to Business Innovation by Building on the Ideas of Others.* New York: Gotham Press & Penguin Books, 2009.

Reichheld, Fred. The Ultimate Question: Driving Good Profits and True Growth. Boston, MA: Harvard Business School Press, 2006.

Taleb, Nassim Nichlaos. *The Black Swain: The Impact of the Highly Improbable.* New York: Random House, 2007.

Turner, Kevin. *Change is Good: Creating Opportunity Amidst Uncertainty.* Texas: Ashley Down Business Press, 2011.

Whiteley, Richard C. *The Customer-Driven Company: Moving From Talk to Action.* Reading, MA: Perseus Books, 1991.

Change

Blanchard, Ken, and John Britt. *Who Killed Change?: Solving the Mystery of Leading People Through Change.* New York: William Morrow; An Imprint of HarperCollins, 2009.

Gerstner, Louis V. Jr. *Who Says Elephants Can't Dance: Leading a*

Great Enterprise Through Dramatic Change. New York: Harper-Collins, 2002.

Harvard Business Review. *Change: Harvard Business Review on Change*. Cambridge, MA: Harvard Business School Press, 1991, 1993, 1995, 1996, 1997, 1998.

Heath, Chip, and Dan Heath. *Switch: How to Change Things When Change is Hard*. New York: Broadway Books, 2010.

Lajoux, Alexandra Reed. *The Art of M&A Integration: A Guide to Merging Resources, Processes & Responsibilities*. New York: McGraw-Hill 2006.

Patterson, Kerry, Joseph Grenny, David Maxfield, Ron McMillan, and Al Switzler. *Influencer: The Power to Change Anything*. New York: McGraw-Hill, 2008.

Phillips, Jack J. Ph.D., and Ron Drewstone. *How to Measure Training Results: The Practical Guide to Tracking the Six Key Indicators*. New York: McGraw-Hill, 2002.

Turner, Kevin. *Change is Good: Creating Opportunity Amidst Uncertainty*. Texas: Ashley Down Business Press, 2011.

Classics

Bettger, Frank. *How I Raised Myself from Failure to Success in Selling*. New York: Simon & Schuster, 1949.

Carnegie, Dale. *Effective Speaking: The Quick and Easy Way*. New York: Dale Carnegie & Associates, 1962.

Carnegie, Dale. *How to Win Friends & Influence People*. New York: Simon & Schuster, 1936, 1964.

Covey, Stephen R. *The 7 Habits of Highly Effective People*. New York: Simon & Schuster, 1989.

Hammer, Michael, and James Champy. *Reengineering the Corporation: A Manifesto for Business Revolution*. New York: HarperCollins, 1993.

Hill, Napoleon. *Think and Grow Rich*. Greenwich, Conn: Fawcett

Publications, 1937.

MacKay, Harvey. *Swim With the Sharks*. New York: William Morrow, 1988.

Consulting

Bower, Marvin. *The Will to Lead: Running a Business with a Network of Leaders*. Boston, MA: Harvard Business school Press, 1997.

Bower, Marvin. *The Will to Manage: Corporate Success Through Programmed Management*. New York: McGraw-Hill, 1966.

Edersheim, Elizabeth Haas. *McKinsey's Marvin Bower: Vision, Leadership & the Creation of Management Consulting*. New York: John Wiley & Sons, 2004.

Friga, Paul N. Ph.D. *The McKinsey Engagement: A Powerful Toolkit for more Efficient & Effective Team Problem Solving*. New York: McGraw-Hill, 2009.

Kiechel, Walter, III. *The Lords of Strategy: The Secret Intellectual History of the New Corporate World*. Boston, MA: Harvard Business School Press, 2010.

Rasiel, Ethan M. *The McKinsey Way: Using the Techniques of the World's Top Strategic Consultants to Help You and Your Business*. New York: McGraw-Hill, 1999.

Turner, Kevin. *Change is Good: Creating Opportunity Amidst Uncertainty*. Texas: Ashley Down Business Press, 2011.

Executive Presence

Baldrige, Letitia. *Lititia Baldrige's New Complete Guide to Executive Manners*. New York: Rawson Associates, 1985, 1993.

Casperson, Dana May. *Power Etiquette: What You Don't Know Can Kill Your Career*. New York: AMACOM, American Management Association, 1999.

Monarth, Harrison. *Executive Presence: The Art of Commanding Respect Like a CEO*. New York: McGraw-Hill, 2010.

Parkhurst, William. *The Eloquent Executive: A Guide to High-Impact Speaking in Big Meetings, Small Meetings, and One-on-One.* New York: Times Books, 1988.

Wall Street Journal. *The Wall Street Journal Book of Chief Executive Style: Amenities and Customs of America's Corporate Elite.* New York: William Morrow and Co., 1989.

History, Business

Cannadine, David. *Mellon: An American Life.* New York: Alfred A. Knopf, 2006.

Carnegie, Andrew. *The Autobiography of Andrew Carnegie.* New York: Penguin Group, 2006.

Chernow, Ron. *The House of Morgan: An American Banking Dynasty and the Rise of Modern Finance.* New York: Atlantic Monthly Press, 1990.

Ellis, Joseph J. *Founding Brothers: The Revolutionary Generation.* New York: Vintage Books, 2000

Fraser, Steve. *Every Man a Speculator: A History of Wall Street in American Life.* New York: HarperCollins Publishers, 2005.

Gordon, John Steele. *An Empire of Wealth: The Epic History of American Economic Power.* New York: HarperCollins Publishers, 2004.

Isaacson, Walter. *Benjamin Franklin: An American Life.* New York: Simon & Schuster, 2003.

Johnson, Paul E.. *A Shopkeeper's Millennium: Society and Revival in Rochester, New York, 1815-1837.* New York: Hill and Wang, 1978, 2004.

Kaplan, Justin. *When the Astors Owned New York: Blue Bloods and Grand Hotels in a Gilded Age.* New York: Viking Penguin, 2006.

McCullough, David. *1776.* New York: Simon & Schuster, 2005.

Nasaw, David. Andrew Carnegie. New York: Penguin Press, 2006.

Phillips, Donald T. *The Founding Fathers on Leadership: Classic Teamwork in Changing Times.* New York: Warner Books, 1997.

Phillips, Donald T. *Lincoln on Leadership: Executive Strategies for Tough Times*. New York: Warner Books, 1993.

Renehan, Edward J. Jr. *Commodore: The Life of Cornelius Vanderbilt*. New York: Perseus Books Group, 2007.

Slack, Charles. *Hetty: The Genius and Madness of America's First Female Tycoon*. New York: Harper Collins Publishers, 2004.

Strouse, Jean. *Morgan: American Financier*. New York: Harper Perennial Publishers, 2000.

Leadership

Autry, James A. *The Servant Leader: How to Build a Creative Team, Develop Great Morale, and Improve Bottome-Line Performance*. Roseville, CA: Prima Publishing, 2001.

Blanchard, Ken, and Phil Hodges. *The Servant Leader: Transforming Your Heart, Head, Hands, and Habits*. Nashville, TN: Thomas Nelson, Inc., 2003.

Bossidy, Larry, and Ram Charan. *Confronting Reality: Doing What Matters to Get Things Right*. New York: Crowne Business Books, 2004.

Brinker, Norman, and Donald T. Phillips. *On The Brink: The Life and Leadership of Norman Brinker*. Texas: Summit, 1996.

Camp, Jim. *Start with No*. New York: Crowne Publishing, 2002.

Cialdini, Robert B. Ph.D. *Influence: The Psychology of Persuasion*. New York: Quill, 1984, 1993.

Charan, Ram, Stephen Drotter, and James Noel. *The Leadership Pipeline: How to Build the Leadership-Powered Company*. New York: Jossey-Bass, A John Wiley Company, 2001.

Cohen, Allan R., and David L. Bradford. *Influence without Authority: The Way to Get Things Done at Work*. New York: John Wiley & Sons, 1989, 1991.

Colvin, Geoff. *Talent is Overrated: What Really Separates World-Class Performers from Everybody Else*. New York: Penguin Books,

2008.

Covey, Stephen R. *The 7 Habits of Highly Effective People.* New York: Simon & Schuster, 1989.

Finkelstein, Sydney. *Why Smart Executives Fail: And What You Can Learn from Their Mistakes.* New York: Penguin Portfolio Trade, 2004.

Fischer, Peter. *The New Boss: How to Survive the First 100 Days.* London: Kogan-Page, 2007.

Gerstner, Louis V. Jr. *Who Says Elephants Can't Dance: Leading a Great Enterprise Through Dramatic Change.* New York: Harper-Collins, 2002.

Godin, Seth. *Tribes: We Need You to Lead Us.* New York: The Penguin Group; Portfolio, 2008.

Kotter, John P. *Power and Influence: Beyond Formal Authority.* New York: The Free Press, a Division of McMillan, 1985.

Leeds, Dorothy. *The 7 Powers of Questions: Secrets to Successful Communication in Life and at Work.* New York: Penguin Group, 2000.

Lieberman, David J. Ph.D. *Get Anyone to do Anything and Never Feel Powerless Again.* New York: St. Martin's Griffin, 2000.

Lombardi, Vince Jr. *What It Takes to be #1: Vince Lombardi on Leadership.* New York: McGraw-Hill, 2001.

McGarvie, Blythe. *Fit In Stand Out: The Key to Leadership Effectiveness in Business and Life.* New York: McGraw-Hill, 2006.

Mitchell, Jack. *Hug Your People: The Proven Way to Hire, Inspire, and Recognize Your Employees and Achieve Remarkable Results.* New York: Hyperion, 2008.

Parinello, Anthony. *Think and Sell Like a CEO.* Canada: Entrepreneur Press, 2002.

Patterson, Kerry, Joseph Grenny, David Maxfield, Ron McMillan, and Al Switzler. *Influencer: The Power to Change Anything.* New York: McGraw-Hill, 2008.

Pfeffer, Jeffrey, and O'Reilly, Charles A. III. *Hidden Value: How Great Companies Achieve Extraordinary Results with Ordinary People*. Boston, MA: Harvard Business School Press, 2000.

Pfeffer, Jeffrey. *Power: Why Some People Have it – and Others Don't*. New York: HarperCollins, 2010.

Pfeffer, Jeffrey. *The Human Equation: Building Profits by Putting People First*. Boston, MA: Harvard Business School Press, 1998.

Pfeffer, Jeffrey, and Robert I. Sutton. *The Knowing-Doing Gap: How Smart Companies Turn Knowledge into Action*. Boston, MA: Harvard Business School Press, 2000.

Phillips, Jack J. Ph.D., and Ron Drewstone. *How to Measure Training Results: The Practical Guide to Tracking the Six Key Indicators*. New York: McGraw-Hill, 2002.

Phillips, Jack J. Ph.D., Timothy W. Bothell, Ph.D., and G. Lynne Snead. *Crucial Confrontations: Tools for Resolving Broken Promises, Violated Expectations, and Bad Behavior*. New York: McGraw-Hill, 2005.

Phillips, Jack J. Ph.D., Timothy W. Bothell, Ph.D., and G. Lynne Snead. *The Project Management Scorecard: Measuring the Success of Project Management Solutions*. New York: Butterworth-Heinemann, 2002.

Shapiro, Ronald M., and Mark A. Jankowski. *Bullies, Tyrants, and Impossible People*. New York: Crown Business, 2005.

Simons, Tony. *The Integrity Dividend: Leading by The Power of Your Word*. New York: Jossey-Bass, 2008.

Surowiecki, James. *The Wisdom of Crowds: Why the Many are Smarter than the Few and How Collective Wisdom Shapes Business, Economies, Societies, and Nations*. New York: Doubleday, 2004.

Turner, Kevin. *Change is Good: Creating Opportunity Amidst Uncertainty*. Texas: Ashley Down Business Press, 2011.

Tutelman, Cary J., and Larry D. Hause. *The Balance Point: New Ways Business Owners Can Use Boards*. Edina, Minn.: Famillepress, 2008.

Weissman, Jerry. *Presenting to Win: The Art of Telling Your Story*.

Upper Saddle River, NJ: FT Press, 2006.

Wiseman, Liz. *Multipliers: How the Best Leaders Make Everyone Smarter.* New York: HarperCollins, 2010.

Wooden, John. *Wooden on Leadership.* New York: McGraw-Hill, 2005.

M&A's and Start-Ups

BenDaniel, David J., and Arthur H. Rosenbloom. *Doing the Deal: International M&A Joint Ventures & Beyond.* New York: John Wiley & Sons, 1998.

Brodsky, Norm, and Bo Burlingham. *The Knack: How Street-Smart Entrepreneurs Learn to Handle Whatever Comes Up.* New York: Penguin Group, 2008.

Cain, Gordon. *Everybody Wins!: A Life in Free Enterprise.* Philadelphia: Chemical Heritage Press, 2001.

Eccles, Robert G., and Dwight B. Crane. *Doing Deals: Investment Banks at Work.* Boston, MA: Harvard Business Press, 1988.

Fuqua, J.B. *Fuqua: How I Made My Fortune Using Other People's Money.* Atlanta: Longstreet Press, 2001.

Harman, Sidney. *Mind Your Own Business: A Maverick's Guide to Business, Leadership and Life.* New York: Double Day, 2003.

Hooke, Jeffrey C. *M&A: A Practical guide to Doing the Deal.* New York: John Wiley & Sons, 1997.

Kawasaki, Guy. *The Art of The Start: Time-Tested, Battle-Hardened Guide for Anyone Starting Anything.* New York: Penguin Group, 2004.

Lajoux, Alexandra Reed. *The Art of M&A Integration: A Guide to Merging Resources, Processes & Responsibilities.* New York: McGraw-Hill 2006.

Magee, David. *Turnaround: How Carlos Ghosn Rescued Nissan.* New York: HarperCollins, 2003.

McQueen, Rod. *Blackberry: The Inside Story of Research In Motion*. Toronto, Ontario, Canada: Key Porter Books, 2010.

Miller, Steve. *The Turnaround Kid: What I Learned Rescuing America's Most Troubled Companies*. New York: HarperCollins, 2008.

Pachter, Barbara. *When the Little Things Count . . . And They Always Count: 601 Essential Things That Everyone in Business Needs to Know*. New York: Marlowe & Co., 2001, 2006.

Rickertsen, Rick. *Buyout: The Insider's Guide to Buying Your Own Company*. New York: AMACOM, American Management Association, 2001.

Rye, David E., and Craig R. Hickman. *Starting Up: Do You Have What it Takes to Make it in Your Own Business?* Paramus, NJ: Prentice Hall Press, 1997.

Turner, Kevin. *Change is Good: Creating Opportunity Amidst Uncertainty*. Texas: Ashley Down Business Press, 2011.

Wyly, Sam. *1,000 Dollars & An Idea: Entrepreneur to Billionaire*. New York: New Market Press, 2008.

Networking

Ferrazzi, Keith. *Who's Got Your Back: The Breakthrough Program to Build Deep, Trusting Relationships that Create Success – And Won't Let You Fail*. New York: Broadway Books, 2009.

Frishman, Rick, and Jill Lublin. *Networking Magic: Finding the Best*. Avon, MA: Adams Media, 2004.

Iacoboni, Marco. *Mirroring People: The New Science of How We Connect with Others*. New York: Farrar, Straus, and Giroux, 2008.

Laird, Pamela Walker. *Pull: Networking and Success since Benjamin Franklin*. Cambridge, MA: Harvard University Press.

Paul, Marla. *The Friendship Crisis: Finding, Making, and Keeping Friends When You're Not a Kid Anymore*. Emmaus, Pennsylvania: Rodale Press, 2004.

Watts, Duncan J. *Six Degrees: The Science of a Connected Age*. New York: W.W. Norton, 2003.

Sales & Development

Alessandra, Tony, Ph.d., Phil Wexler, and Rick Barrera. *Non-Manipulative Selling: Strategies & Techniques for Creating Customers, Not Just Sales*. New York: Prentice Hall Press, 1987.

Bettger, Frank. *How I Raised Myself from Failure to Success in Selling*. New York: Simon & Schuster, 1949.

Boylan, Michael A. *Accelerants: 12 Strategies to Sell Faster, Close Deals Faster, and Grow Business Faster*. New York: Penguin Group, 2007.

Brem, Marion Luna. *Women Make the Best Salesmen*. New York: Double Day, 2004.

Fisher, Roger, William L. Ury, and Bruce Patton. *Getting to Yes: Negotiating Agreement Without Giving In*. New York: Penguin, 1991.

Freese, Thomas A. *Secrets of Question-Based Selling: How the Most Powerful Tool in Business Can Double Your Sales Results*. Naperville, IL: Sourcebooks, Inc., 2000, 2003.

Harding, Ford. *Creating Rainmakers: The Manager's Guide to Training Professionals to Attract New Clients*. New York: John Wiley & Sons, 2006.

Harding, Ford. *Rain-Making: Attracting New Clients*. Holbrook, MA: Adams Media Corp., 1994.

Hogan, Kevin. *The Science of Influence: How to Get Anyone to Say Yes in 8 minutes or Less!*. New York: John Wiley & Sons, 2005.

Leeds, Dorothy. *The 7 Powers of Questions: Secrets to Successful Communication in Life and at Work*. New York: Penguin Group, 2000.

Lindstrom, Martin. *Buy-ology: Truth and Lies About Why We Buy*. New York: Double Day, 2008.

Miller, Robert B., and Stephen E. Heiman. *Strategic Selling: The Unique Sales System Proven Successful by America's Best Companies*. New York: Warner Books, 1985.

Miller, Robert B., and Stephen E. Heiman. *The New Strategic Selling: The Unique Sales System Proven Successful by America's Best Companies.* New York: Warner Books, 1998.

Mitchell, Jack. *Hug Your Customers: The Proven Way to Personalize Sales and Achieve Astounding Results.* New York: Hyperion, 2003.

Parinello, Anthony. *Think and Sell Like a CEO.* Canada: Entrepreneur Press, 2002.

Rackham, Neil. *Major Account Sales Strategy.* New York: McGraw-Hill, 1989.

Rackham, Neil, and John DeVincentis. *Rethinking the Sales Force: Redefining Selling to Create and Capture Customer Value.* New York" McGraw-Hill, 1999.

Rackham, Neil. *Spin Selling.* New York: McGraw-Hill, 1988.

Reichheld, Fred. The Ultimate Question: Driving Good Profits and True Growth. Boston, MA: Harvard Business School Press, 2006.

Schwartz, Barry. *The Paradox of Choice: Why More is Less.* New York: Harper Perennial, 2004.

Turner, Kevin. *Change is Good: Creating Opportunity Amidst Uncertainty.* Texas: Ashley Down Business Press, 2011.

Ury, William. *Getting Past No: Negotiating with Difficult People.* New York: Bantam Books, 1991.

Watts, Duncan J. *Six Degrees: The Science of a Connected Age.* New York: W.W. Norton, 2003.

Weissman, Jerry. *Presenting to Win: The Art of Telling Your Story.* Upper Saddle River, NJ: FT Press, 2006.
>>>>>>>>>>>>>>>>>>>>>>>>>>>

Strategy

Boston Consulting Group. *On Strategy: Cash Cows, Experience Curves, Time-Based Competition, Richness and Reach, and Other BCG Ideas.* New York: John Wiley & Sons, 2006.

Goldstein, Leonard, Timothy Nolan, and J. William Pfeiffer. *Applied Strategic Planning: How to Develop a Plan That Really Works.*

New York: McGraw-Hill, 1993.

Porter, Michael E. *Competitive Strategy: Techniques for Analyzing Industries and Competitors*. New York: The Free Press, a Division of MacMillan Publishing Company, 1980.

Porter, Michael E. *On Competition.* Boston, MA: Harvard Business Review Book, 1998.

Porter, Michael E., Cynthia A. Montgomery, and Harvard Business Review. *Strategy: Seeking and Securing Competitive Advantage.* Boston, MA: Harvard Business School Press, 1979, 1980, 1981, 1983-1991.

Robert, Michel. *Strategy: Pure & Simple*. New York: McGraw-Hill, 1993.

Robert, Michel. *The Power of Strategic Thinking: Lock in Markets, Lock Out Competitors.* New York: McGraw-Hill, 2000.

Turner, Kevin. *Change is Good: Creating Opportunity Amidst Uncertainty.* Texas: Ashley Down Business Press, 2011.

General

Brett, Jeanne. *Negotiating Globally: How to Negotiate Deals, Resolve Disputes, and Make Decisions Across Cultural Boundaries*. San Francisco: Jossey-Bass, 2007.

Buckingham, Marcus, and Donald O. Clifton, Ph.D. Now, Discover Your Strengths. New York: The Free Press – Simon & Schuster, 2001.

Greenberg, Herb, Harold Weinstein, and Patrick Sweeney. *How to Hire & Develop Your Next Your Next Top Performer: The Five Qualities That Make Salespeople Great.* New York: McGraw-Hill, 2001.

Gubman, Edward L. *The Talent Solution: Aligning Strategy and People to Achieve Extraordinary Results.* New York: McGraw-Hill, 1998.

Mlodinow, Leonard. *The Drunkard's Walk: How Randomness Rules Our Lives*. New York: Pantheon Books, 2008.

Smartt, Geoff, and Randy Street. *Who: Solve Your #1 Problem –*

When I Have A Granddaughter

(closing excerpt from the Keynote speech "Change is Good" by Kevin Turner)
Change can be a scary thing. So when I have a granddaughter, instead of "grandfather" she's going to call me Pa. Because I called my grandfather Pa. And I always knew that no matter what happened, Pa was ALWAYS there for me.

And there is one thing we know we can ALL depend on and that's CHANGE. And the first time she realizes that whether she likes it or not, change is coming , I'll make sure she knows she doesn't have to weather that storm alone.

Because change can be a scary thing, especially when you have to endure it alone. But no matter how wide the approaching storm appears to be, I will remind her that "this too shall pass." Because like all storms; storms come and storms go. Nothing lasts forever.

And "Sweetheart," I will tell her, "Don't think the approaching storm won't affect you. Because it will. It will change you. But it will change you for the better because storms have a way of cleansing the air of all that makes life reek.

And remember that after the storm you will want to reach out and fill your lungs to capacity with the fresh air that comes after a cleansing rain. Because it is the fresh new air that reminds you that 'all things are possible,' that the hopes and dreams you've held on to for so long can now take root, and grow – to unforeseen heights, and at dizzying speeds, if only you will allow them."

I want her to see the storms in life for what they really are; opportunities for growth and change.

"And Sweetheart," I'll tell her, "Don't you get too comfortable with today because today's comforts lead to complacency. And complacency is always a painful death of the senses – of everything that's important to you. Instead, fix your sites on tomorrow. And with passion and enthusiasm, embrace the changes that always come with tomorrow. For with tomorrow always comes a new opportunity, if only you will get up off of your comfort zone and pursue change!"

By Kevin Turner, author of
Change is Good

* REAL PRIORITIES

* TIME MANAGEMENT

* DILIGENCE WITH DISCIPLINE

* DAILY OBJECTIVES BASED
  ON GOALS